The Elements of Graphology

Barry Branston trained under the personal tuition of Joan Cambridge, Britain's foremost handwriting psychologist. He qualified as a scientific graphologist in 1977. A founder member of the Graphology Society, he lectures extensively and writes numerous articles on the subject.

The *Elements of* is a series designed to present high quality intro-
ductions to a broad range of essential subjects.

The books are commissioned specifically from experts in their
fields. They provide readable and often unique views of the various
topics covered, and are therefore of interest both to those who have
some knowledge of the subject, as well as to those who are
approaching it for the first time.

Many of these concise yet comprehensive books have practical sug-
gestions and exercises which allow personal experience as well as
theoretical understanding, and offer a valuable source of information on many important themes.

In the same series

THE ELEMENTS OF

GRAPHOLOGY

Barry Branston

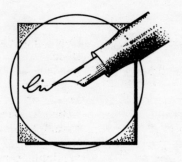

ELEMENT

Shaftesbury, Dorset ● Rockport, Massachusetts
Brisbane, Queensland

First published in Great Britain in 1995 by
Element Books Limited
Shaftesbury, Dorset SP7 8BP

Published in the USA in 1995 by
Element Books, Inc.
42 Broadway, Rockport, MA 01966

Published in Australia in 1995 by
Element Books Limited
for Jacaranda Wiley Limited
33 Park Road, Milton, Brisbane 4064

Cover design by Max Fairbrother
Designed and typeset by Linda Reed and Joss Nizan
Printed and bound in Great Britain by
Biddles Ltd, Guildford and King's Lynn

British Library Cataloguing in Publication
data available

Library of Congress Cataloging in Publication
data available

ISBN 1-85230-646-7

I dedicate this book to my wife, Olivia,
who has had the awesome task of interpreting
my fast, almost illegible handwriting.

NOTE TO THE READER

All measurements in this book are given in millimetres. You can find approximate equivalents in inches using the following table.

millimetres	inches (approximate)
5mm	0.2 inch
8mm	0.3 inch
10mm	0.4 inch
13mm	0.5 inch
18mm	0.7 inch
20mm	0.8 inch
23mm	0.9 inch
25mm	1.0 inch

CONTENTS

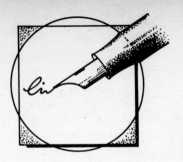

INTRODUCTION
What is Graphology?

Graphology, sometimes called handwriting analysis, is the study of handwriting with the aim of revealing the character and personality of the writer and his or her strengths, weaknesses and abilities.

Psychological methods (psychometric tests) have been developed, particularly for industry, to ascertain the personality of potential recruits and probe the inner secrets of their characters. These tests are taken by the applicants under supervision, and their answers to specific questions are then evaluated. However, the recruits have to be there in person and may know what is expected of them. Graphology has no such fetters. It can be carried out anywhere, by mailing the candidate's handwritten letter of application to the graphologist and awaiting his or her report. The candidates will no doubt be aware that their handwriting is being examined and should have no fear of this being done. The assessment must, however, be carried out by a fully experienced analyst who is conversant with the industry concerned and who has a basic understanding of psychology as well as a practical knowledge of people.

Handwriting springs from the unconscious and contains a great deal of information which can form the basis of character interpretation. Each time we write we are under

1

the influence of inner feelings and emotions that dictate our mood at the time of writing. Handwriting is, in fact, 'brain-writing' which transmits instructions through the motor nervous system to the hand holding the pen. These instructions make the fingers expand and contract to produce writing. This is an expressive movement, a mixture of conscious thought and unconscious automatic responses to stimulation learned as a part of bodily movement. An individual's hand-writing is as unique as his or her voice pattern and finger-prints: no two are exactly alike.

We therefore produce a graphic picture of ourselves every time we put pen to paper, and a graphologist can interpret this picture in terms of personality expression and character – not only the way the writer wishes to be seen, but how he or she really is. Of course a piece of writing can be studied at any time after it has been written, whether after 2 minutes or 200 years, as in the case of historical documents. And since an individual's personality changes over time, these changes can be studied in handwriting samples, for instance to help in a biography or in the case of a disputed will.

Learning to do this takes time, but I hope this book will help you. Graphology is a way of fully understanding friends, colleagues and relatives, or indeed anyone whose handwriting you can examine, and of discovering the way they think – whether by logic, intuition or both. It can also highlight behavioural characteristics such as argumentative tendencies and aggression, an ostentatious manner which perhaps compensates for feelings of inferiority, genuine friendliness and emotional control, conventional habits, manipulation or jealousy, so paving the way for a more rewarding relationship. You will also come across indications of intimate habits and personal details which should, of course, be kept confidential.

You may ask, 'Can anyone be a graphologist?' The answer is yes, particularly if you are interested in people and have a fair ability for observation and deductive perception. It depends of course upon how deeply you want to go into the subject – whether merely for interest or as a serious study.

People will tell you that their handwriting changes. Yes, of course it does: it depends upon how you are feeling at the time of writing – depression, optimism, happiness, anxiety and other emotional states will affect the script slightly. But the basic structure is unlikely to change. If you suspect that it has changed, ask for another sample of writing written at a time when the writer was not under the influence of extraordinary conditions. A memorandum to oneself or a diary entry will also look different from a letter of application for a job. And of course, as a person progresses through life, any mental or emotional changes will gradually be reflected in his or her writing over the years. A 'copybook' writer, who adheres to the basic form of letters as taught at school, may say, 'I write as my teacher did.' But the teacher will undoubtedly have been writing copybook forms for clarity rather than as their natural style.

You cannot tell, except by intuition, whether a piece of writing is by a man or woman. There are feminine men and masculine women. So although masculinity and femininity will be revealed in the script, it is imperative to ask for the sex of the writer, unless of course it is obvious from the content or signature. Age cannot be ascertained through handwriting either. Some people are mature at an early age while others are still immature at an advanced age.

Graphology cannot foretell the future, nor is it a way of telling the writer's fortune, but it can point to the way they are progressing – or not. Nor will it reveal what the writer actually does as an occupation or profession. It may tell you what they should be doing, but many people are in jobs for which they are not suited while their actual inclinations and abilities lie elsewhere. And, of course, a person's colour is not evident in his or her script.

HISTORY OF GRAPHOLOGY

It is not my intention to delve too deeply into the history of handwriting analysis, but it is interesting to know that it has been in existence for a very long time. In the 2nd century the Roman historian Suetonius Tranquillus concluded that the handwriting of Augustus Caesar was not separated sufficiently to read plainly and that he was therefore mean. Nero also deduced from the writing of one of his officers that he was untrustworthy. Ancient Chinese philosophers could distinguish the distinct writing style of certain calligraphers and made deductions regarding their characters.

But it was in Italy during the early part of the 17th century that Alderisius Prosper wrote the first known article on the subject called 'Ideographia'. This was followed in 1622 by a slim volume on how to tell a person's nature by his or her handwriting, written by Camillo Baldo, a physician in Capri. This book was probably used by entertainers who travelled from castle to castle giving character readings.

Very little attention was paid to handwriting analysis during the next 100 years or so. Later, the subject captured the attention of writers such as Balzac, Lavater, Goethe, Edgar Allen Poe, Elizabeth Barrett Browning and Charles Dickens, all of whom began to use handwriting analysis with accuracy. Other known handwriting analysts were George Sand, Robert Browning, Chekhov and Albert Einstein; there was also Sir William Herschel, the father of the science of fingerprinting. We know too that the artist Gainsborough kept on the side of his easel a sample of the handwriting of the person whose portrait he was painting.

It was in about 1830 that handwriting analysis really took off in France, when a group of senior ecclesiastical men became seriously interested in the subject. They were the Archbishop of Cambrai, Bishop Soudinet of Amiens, Cardinal Regnier, and Abbé Louis Flandrin (1808–81), who taught handwriting analysis. And it was with his pupil, the Abbé Jean-Hippolyte Michon of Paris, that the serious investigative study of handwriting analysis really began. Indeed, it was he who, in 1871, coined the name 'Graphology' meaning roughly 'knowledge of writing'. He published a book in 1872 called *Les Mystères de l'Ecriture* and this was followed by *La Méthode Pratique de Graphologie*. These volumes provided the basis for further research and led to the establishment of the first graphology society in Paris.

Michon, however, made no connection between graphology and psychology, and he was later known as an interpreter of fixed signs. He compared thousands of handwriting samples with what was known about the writers, and listed the graphic details common to people with the same qualities. He made a very extensive list of signs, each of which related to the forms of the letters and had a fixed meaning. He believed that the presence of a certain sign in the writing meant that whatever that sign represented in terms of personality or character was to be found in that writer. If the sign was absent then so was the quality it represented. We are now aware that this does not give an accurate assessment. We need to validate the form with a confirming movement; the findings must be co-ordinated as a whole, as was discovered by Jules Crépieux-Jamin (1858–1940), a French physician and psychologist. However, the valuable work Michon did set the scene for subsequent research.

Crépieux-Jamin published many books, but the most important was *L'ABC de la Graphologie*, published in 1929, which was the result of his extensive studies. He then enlisted the help of Alfred Binet, the inventor of the IQ test, who had himself studied and researched graphology at the Sorbonne, to report on his findings. Binet related it to psychological testing with respect to intelligence and integrity and found it reliable, thereby giving graphology further credibility and generating further research by his enthusiasm.

In about 1880, three German doctors approached the subject from a psychological standpoint and published their extensive research. One of them, Ludwig Klages (1872–1956), a physicist, philosopher and psychologist, became a leading graphologist. It was he who created Form Level (the overall standard of the writing – see *chapter 6*), the basic quality of a handwriting which plays an essential part in the compilation of an assessment, and in the decision whether a positive or negative interpretation is to be applied. Klages also researched in great depth the rhythmic quality of handwriting – speed, spacing and pressure – putting it on a more scientific basis. With Hans Busse he founded the German Graphological Society in Munich and edited a periodical which brought graphologists of the day together and featured at length the various graphological discoveries that had taken place. Most of the readers were, of course, amateurs since graphology was still in its infancy.

Another of the three Germans, Dr William Preyer, conducted research into signatures and found that they relate to how people see themselves and how they want others to see them, and should not be assessed without a sample of the writer's script to hand, because the two can be at variance. He worked with soldiers who had lost their writing hands and he discovered that the basic structure of the writing they produced with the other hand or, when both hands had been lost, with their mouths or feet, had not altered. He therefore declared that handwriting was really 'brainwriting'.

The third doctor, George Meyer, investigated the meaning of writing movement, speed and pressure, and the relationship between writing and emotional reaction. He also distinguished between spontaneous (natural) writing and unspontaneous (unnatural) writing in graphically mature writers, which is valuable where a document is suspected of being forged. He looked into initial (beginning) strokes and terminal (end) strokes and what they represented in terms of the mental preparation the writer needed before starting and continuing a task without interruption of thought.

Speed was also an important consideration for Robert Saudek of Czechoslovakia who emigrated to Britain in about 1925. He did research into how a writer is influenced by the school copybook style he or she is first taught and how this style is modified into a unique, personal form by the writer over the years.

Saudek was particularly interested in how handwriting in Britain differed from Continental styles, especially in relation to the use of block capitals instead of script for official and commercial names and addresses. His book *The Psychology of Handwriting* was published in 1925, and reprinted in 1954. It was written in the hope that national handwriting tendencies would create a common ground for further investigation into what he termed 'the new science of Graphology'.

The great Swiss graphologist, Dr Max Pulver (1899–1952), a philosopher at the University of Zurich and an associate of the psychologist Dr Carl Jung, conducted research into the symbolism of space (margins and the space between lines and words). In 1931 he wrote a famous book entitled *Symbolik der Handschrift* (now available in English as *The Symbolism of Handwriting* – see *Further Reading*), in which psychology is extensively featured. He extended Klages's system of graphology and introduced a third dimension, depth (pressure), in addition to vertical and horizontal movements. He also made a study of the graphological signs of lying or economy with the truth in relation to speed.

He also applied psychology to the upper, middle and lower zones, explaining that in fulfilling the purpose of communication, each movement is directed towards the other person and, as it originates in the Ego (real self) and is directed from the I to the you, the writing movement shows the path of expression. It is the bridge of communication. According to the character of the writer each movement will go in either a straightforward direction or will make detours through the upper and lower parts of the script with a tendency to waste time and effort.

Graphology did not really make headway in the UK until 1936 when H J Jacoby arrived from Germany and published his main work entitled *Handwriting Analysis: An Introduction into Scientific Graphology*, the first book to use photographs of the handwriting examples. Then in 1938 Dr Eric Singer, a Doctor of Law from the University of Virginia, moved to London, where he opened a graphology practice, specializing in recruitment and marriage compatibility. His research included ego symbols, ie the personal pronoun 'I' (PPI). He wrote three books which were condensed into one in 1969, under the title *A Manual of Graphology*.

There were also a few notable American graphologists, including Philip Vernon and Gordon Allport of the Harvard Clinic of Psychology. Also of note was Dr Ulrich Sonnemann, Professor at the School of Social Research in New York. He made a serious study of clinical psychology, including schizophrenia, in his book *Handwriting Analysis as A Psychodiagnostic Tool*, which was published in 1950, and carried out a critical revision of Ludwig Klages's graphological principles, suggesting a way in which they could be further developed.

Another American pioneer was June Downey, of the University of Iowa, who worked on the expressive movement of handwriting.

Marie Bernard was born in Berlin and became a famous classical singer. She moved to New York when her husband died, but later moved back to Germany, where she studied graphology, and qualified at Munich University. In 1976, the President of the American Society of Handwriting Analysts invited her to return to the United States to teach graphology and translate European graphological authors into English. So she taught graphology at City College, New York and Bridgeport University. She has written 15 books on the subject. *The Art of Graphology* and *Sex in Handwriting* are particulary highly recommended.

Also recommended are the books by the late Patricia Marne, who died in 1992. She was a founder member of the Graphology Society in the UK. She was a personal friend and colleague of mine and also taught my wife Olivia. By profession, she was a freelance journalist as well as a noted graphologist and was especially well known to the media as a result of her articles in newspapers and magazines. Two of her best known books are *Graphology* and *Crime and Sex in Handwriting* (see *Further Reading*). She was taught graphology at the American School of Contemporary Studies, New York. She also specialized in children's handwriting.

The history of graphological research cannot be concluded without mention of my tutor, the late Joan Cambridge, who died in February 1989, and who was Chairman of the professional organization Scientific Graphologists (England). She was also a handwriting consultant and a member of the Scientific Council, the European Society for Handwriting Psychology. Her main work involved handicapped children. She was recognized as one of the leading graphologists in Europe and worked for many well-known companies as a recruitment specialist.

She worked on the handwriting problems of children with spina bifida, hydrocephalis and autism. With the help of

Dr Elizabeth M Anderson, a senior research officer at the Coram Research Unit, University of London Institute of Education, she devised writing patterns to encourage finger dexterity and control and to give the children expressive outlets in the form of 'scribble-talk'. This has a meaning for the children, who would then read their scribbles out if invited to do so. They eventually made progress towards developing letterforms and stroke structuring.

There are a number of other notable graphologists who have written books which are worthy of attention. These are listed in the *Further Reading* section.

UNDERTAKING AN ANALYSIS

Before describing each element of graphology it is necessary to outline the requirements for an analysis. The sample of handwriting must be written on plain paper, with a ballpoint or fountain pen rather than a pencil or felt-tipped pen; it should preferably be not less than 12 lines long, and include a signature. You must also know the age and sex of the writer, and preferably the nationality and in which country they were taught to write. The reason we need to know the sex of the writer beforehand is that there are men with feminine ways and women with masculine inclinations and sex cannot therefore be judged accurately just from the script, although masculinity and femininity usually can.

It will be helpful to have samples of writing carried out at different times to ascertain the consistency. Do not accept anything specially written for the analysis – it must be spontaneous. It is therefore best if the writer is not aware that his or her writing is being assessed by a graphologist. The reason for this is that writers who know that their handwriting is to be examined will concentrate on the penmanship rather than on producing an unconscious movement which allows the true personality to emerge. There are, in fact, times when a writer needs to project an image, for instance in a job application. In such cases, the beginning of the letter will be written very carefully and slowly, but after the first few lines, when the writer begins to think about *what* he or she is writing as opposed to *how*, the script will become more natural and this will allow for a more accurate appraisal.

The instruments needed for graphology are few: a good-quality magnifying glass, a plastic ruler showing millimetres, and a protractor for accurately assessing the slant. You also need a file in which to keep all the handwriting samples you will collect over the years; and you need a ringbinder and paper for your workbook, in which you will note all the findings and information you will collect. I suggest that you write down all the data you may find useful, preferably under separate headings in the order in which you will compile your worksheet, so that the information will be to hand as you progress, section by section, to the actual analysis. Put in the margin of your workbook the source of the information in case you need to seek further data. It is normal practice to write the positive indications on the left-hand side and the negative ones on the right-hand side, as you will find in most books that give lists of traits (characteristics of personality) as a summary.

It has often been asked whether graphology is an art or a science. The answer is both. The science is in the recognition and measurement of the factors and the art is in the recognition and evaluation of the traits.

I recommend that, if you want to study graphology seriously, you undertake a recognized college course of fundamental psychology, so that you have a full understanding which can provide an objective focus into the whole personality. When you discover that a person is, for instance, an extrovert or an introvert, a basic knowledge of these psychological states is necessary to evaluate the personality characteristics in the final report. Moreover, if more than one specimen of handwriting is available this can be useful to confirm the consistency of the writing. A person who is mentally fully active will tend to have more 'life' (rhythmic quality) in their script than the same person writing late at night and feeling very tired. You could therefore eliminate the risk of being misled by any abnormal influences and conditions under which your sample was written. Never be afraid to ask if another specimen of writing is available.

I suggest that you read this book twice before starting to analyse a few samples of clear and legible writing – and, when you can be objective and honest with yourself, samples of your own. Do not be too ambitious. Build up the basic personality carefully and then, if possible, ask the person whose handwriting you have worked on for their estimate of your efforts. You will make mistakes, but fewer and fewer as you gain experience. Accuracy with just a few facts is far better than a long analysis in which there are mistakes. Except for those who are helping you by giving you samples of handwriting (your findings for which should be kept confidential), do not tell anyone that you are studying graphology until you are quite confident that you have the necessary expertise to take on all comers, because you will be the life and soul of the party when word gets around. On no account tell people only what you think they want to hear. Be honest and straightforward about their weaknesses. I also suggest that you purchase the *Penguin Dictionary of Psychology*, and use it, along with other psychologically orientated books (see *Further Reading*).

You should not under any circumstances provide an analysis of someone's handwriting, either in writing or verbally, without knowing the use to which the appraisal is to be put. It is best to refuse diplomatically and explain your ethical standards; also, never put a name on an analysis, only a code number, which is recognized just by you and the recipient, in case it gets into the wrong hands.

Finally, a word about intuition. After a time you may get certain 'feelings' from the handwriting you are studying. This is an instinctive knowledge without reasoning – an intuitive insight, as if the script is 'talking' to you. Do not dismiss these thoughts – but neither should you add them to your final analysis until you have looked for and found in the writing the characteristic in question.

As you gain more experience, intuition will become a part of your graphological technique, to be used wisely. There are of course those people whose thoughts are purely logical and who would not trust intuitive thought at all. Their handwriting, incidentally, would have a very high upper zone, a sharp

11

stroke, be dominantly connected, with angular forms and probably of small size. The Form Level would be high.

Form Level is fully explained in *chapter 6*. However, to facilitate your understanding, here is a basic description of what it is. You will first assess the writing as it appears to you overall, whether it be harmonious, lively, legible, well organized, clear of blotches and amendments, quickly written. If these features are apparent, you have a medium to high Form Level. If the script is disorganized, with the lines of writing undulating and letters going into one another, a dirty-looking ink line with overloaded, illegible letter formations and extremely heavy pressure in a slow writing, then you have a low Form Level and many of the factors will be on the negative side. But I must point out that it is very rare for all these indications to be seen in one sample; the scripts you will have to examine will mainly be of an average Form Level, with the majority of features on the positive scale.

1 · SCRIPT SIZE AND SLANT

CLUES TO YOUR PERSONALITY

We'll start by looking at some of the most obvious features of a page of handwriting: how big it is and which way it slopes.

ABSOLUTE SIZE

As I have said, I recommend that you read right through the book first, so that, when you are preparing the worksheet on which you will base your analysis (see *chapter 8*), you will understand how we determine the positive and negative interpretations. You will not apply Form Level until the actual personality and character appraisal is ready to be assessed from the indications on your completed worksheet.

The first most noticeable factor on a page of handwriting is the size of the script – whether it is either very large or very small. To ascertain the average size of a script it should be measured: first the overall size, as in the single letter 'f', or a combination of two or three letters which have an upper, middle and lower part, like 'dg' or 'yl'. A normal average size is 9mm (3/8 inch) from top to bottom, and the measurement is taken at 90° upright, regardless of the slant of the writing.

This is *Absolute Size*. If, for instance, the letter 'f' or the combination of letters measures 12mm or 18mm, this is obviously large or very large. Where the size is very inconsistent (irregular), take the majority: thus if there are 2 letters at a height of 17mm, 27 at the height of 12mm and 6 at 4mm, then the average size will be 12mm, because there are more letters of this size than any other. This is your Absolute Size. After you have gained in confidence you will probably know whether you are dealing with a large or small script without actually measuring it. But if you are unsure, then you must use your ruler.

Large writing (see *figure 1*) is associated with an outgoing person with a talent for organizing events, and with leadership qualities needing to be noticed and admired – an extrovert with a need for freedom of expression. Such people would ideally need much space for work and for leisure; needing variety, they would probably have many friends. They would have no time to attend to what would be to them trifling matters; they would need to think expansively.

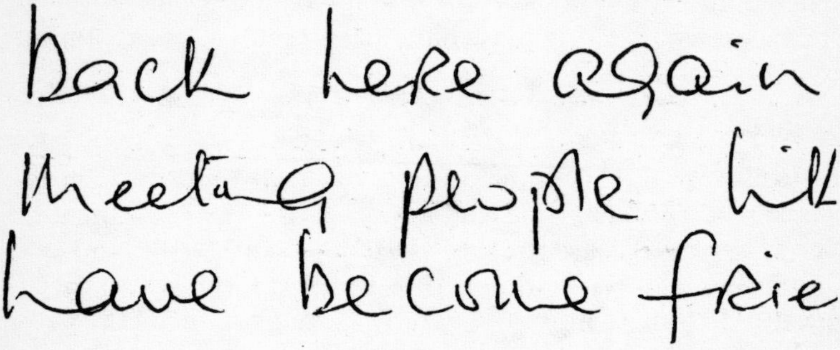

Figure 1

If the Form Level is poor, with ostentatious showy letterforms, then a domineering, inconsiderate person, whose only thought would be to project his or her own image without thinking of others' needs, is indicated. If you have large handwriting, also with a leftward slant and narrow letterforms (introversion), the writer may be putting on a façade of extrovert tendencies which he or she really does not inwardly feel – a compensation.

Small writing (see *figure 2*), say with an average size of less than 7mm, would indicate a matter-of-fact, realistic person with no desire to be in the front line, probably with a job using computers, science or mathematics. These are the professionals, where concentration and accuracy are essential. It is usually found that people with very small writing will have a high Form Level, as there is a need for concentration. However, they can also be fussy and pedantic over details, qualities which often make them difficult to live with, as they will have small but intense fields of interest and can therefore be self-limiting. Often they are not particularly interested in people and have a small circle of friends, chosen from their own occupational area, with whom they can talk 'shop'. Personality projection is not important. They tend to prefer isolation from any outgoing activity. This is not usually due to feelings of inferiority; they just do not like being on show. Their emotional response is usually well balanced and their excitement threshold is always controlled.

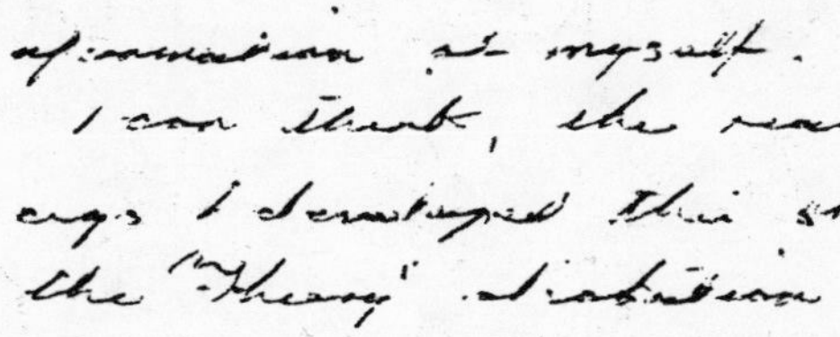

Figure 2

Handwriting that is normal – that is, with an average size of 9mm – will have no special significance other than what will be found in other factors. Such writers are, however, well balanced mentally, socially and sexually, without any aspect being over-indulged. This is particularly true where the script is upright and conventional (with very little originality).

The following tables show the different attributes of large and small writing.

Large Size – over 9mm

Positive	Negative
Self-confident	Arrogant
Optimistic	Domineering
Generous	Vague in relation to
Flexible	concepts
Enthusiastic	Poor at observation
Individualistic	Ostentatious
Possessing leadership qualities	Lacking objectivity
Proud	Lacking accuracy
Idealistic	
Enterprising	
Far-sighted in views and planning	
Likes to be noticed	

Small Size – under 9mm

Positive	Negative
Realistic	Petty
Modest	Fussy
Respectful	Lacking enthusiasm
Peaceful	Fixed in habits
Prudent	Small-minded
Accurate	Lacking self-confidence
Conscientious	
Good at concentration	
Good at observation	
Having a controlled behaviour pattern	
Clever at handling personal resources	

On your worksheet, you will determine the actual size by measurement, if it is not obviously large or small; but you should not add the personality details which are indicated by the size, until you have completed your worksheet.

THE THREE ZONES

In all handwriting there is an upper, middle and lower part. In graphology these three zones are very significant in terms of personality and character expression. Let us now look at the *relative size* of the script in these zones.

We have already seen that the letter 'f' has a normal size of 9mm; however in an adult's handwriting it is seldom that a perfect balance between the three zones is found. One zone may be more dominant than the other two. So even if the absolute measurement is 9mm (normal for the measurement of three zones written in one movement as in the letter 'f'), there could be a considerable disproportion within the separate zones, the normal measurement for each of which is 3mm.

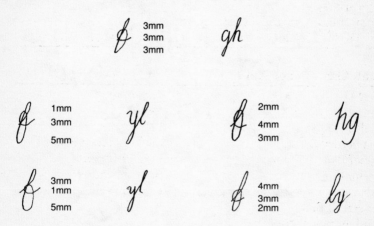

Each zone corresponds to an area of interest. If there is a disproportion (if one zone is higher or lower than 3mm), that indicates that the person is over-active or under-active in that area.

The *upper zone* is the area of the intellect, ambition, spiritual awareness and creative talent. It indicates the degree of thought a writer puts into whatever he or she undertakes, and his or her mental development (see *figure 3*).

The *middle zone* is the area of social relationships, ego demands (what is needed for the inner self) and routine everyday practicality – the domestic and social zone. A very large, dominant middle zone (see *figure 4*) is a sign of immaturity, unless the handwriting is that of an adolescent, who has yet to mature fully.

The *lower zone* is the area of materialistic concern, security values and sexual demands (see *figure 5*; also *figure 7*).

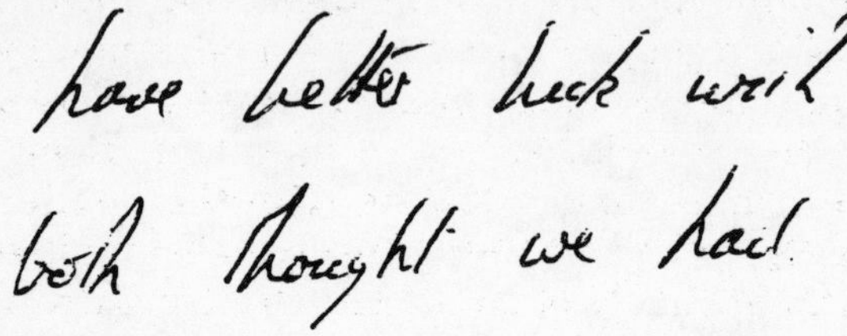

Figure 3

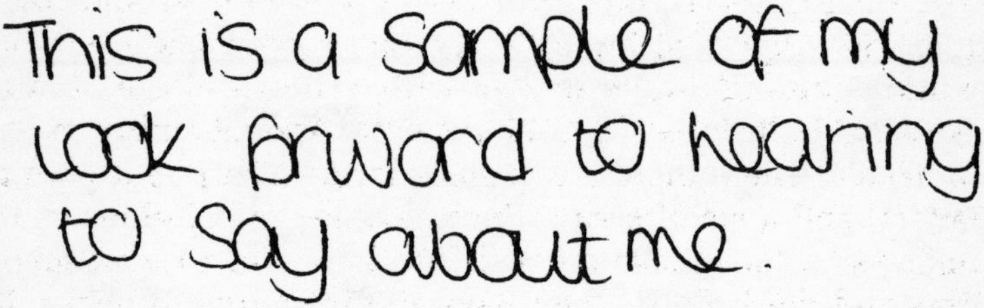

Figure 4

Figure 5

An exaggeration in one zone will mean a lessening of interest in one or both of the other zones, or areas of life. Remember, however, that we should not jump to conclusions without taking into consideration other relevant factors such as the slant, pressure and – particularly with the upper and lower zones – the type of loop or single stroke used.

A dominant upper zone with normal or light pressure will indicate the writer's interest in intellectual subjects. If the pressure is heavy and the middle zone small, with possibly a poor to average Form Level, the person's intellectual ideas are not realistic, because he or she lacks the common sense (as shown by the middle zone) to bring ideas to fruition. A very short upper loop shows a limited response to intellectual subjects – they do not dominate the writer's life.

A large middle zone with small upper and lower zones (see *figure 4*, for example) indicates a feminine mind whose concern is to impress others and who will display strong emotions. I have found this feature prevalent among store demonstrators and women dealing with the public in an advisory capacity. They are always ready to help others, and recognition is always welcome. The more rightward the slant, the more they will naturally relate to others. They have an affinity with most people.

A small middle zone with near normal upper and lower zones (see *figure 6*) indicates a modest personality possibly with feelings of inferiority and with a limited range of interests, particularly in the social sphere. Mental agility is also indicated where there are angular forms (sharp and pointed letters) and a small script. Such people are oblivious to the impression they make on others and are able to plan schedules and work flow. They have the initiative to deal with obstacles as they occur. They also have the ability to deal with the minutiae of life. A very small middle zone can often indicate stress and tension which is not being dissipated in a physical outlet. Such writers are usually found among scientific workers, computer experts, and similar occupations.

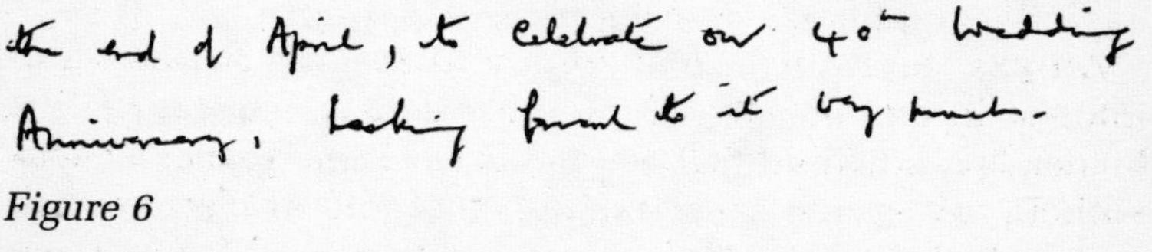

Figure 6

A large lower zone (see *figure 7*), with fair to heavy pressure, indicates a security-conscious individual, with practical inclinations and a healthy need for a physically active life, including a sexual outlet. The degree of imagination (or even fantasy) they put into this will be indicated by the width and fullness of the loops. Where the pressure is light to moderate, it indicates a business-minded individual for whom finance is an important consideration. Where a large lower zone also has exaggerated enrolments or ornamentation, the writer is preoccupied with illusions and dreams, usually of a sexual nature. This feature is also found in the handwriting of homosexuals.

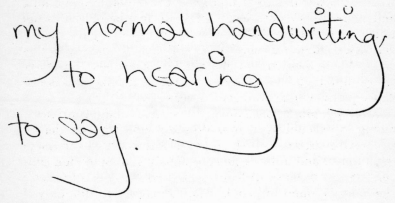

Figure 7

A small lower zone (see *figure 4* on p. 18) indicates moderation in all things physical, and if there is a leftward slant the writer could be fearful of or uninterested in sexual contact. There is also possibly excessive control of emotional responses. The writer with a small lower zone has no inclination towards material possessions, or even towards family interests, and may be thought of as cold, particularly if there is a sharp, thin stroke.

Zonal proportions are the most personal features of handwriting, and the middle zone holds the balance between the upper and lower areas of interest. It is one of the most frequently found clues to forged handwriting. It is very difficult to copy accurately and spontaneously another person's zonal proportions. If you try it yourself, you will see how easy it is to slip into your own zonal measurements. Excessive fluctuation in the size of the zones, particularly with a varied slant and an inconsistent pressure pattern, indicates a person who will have problems coping with life's obstacles. His or her ability to see reason will be impaired.

Sometimes the zonal measurements of the upper and lower zones are the same. Assess where the main focus of interest lies according to where other major extensions occur regularly. For instance, long initial strokes rising from the lower zone or long final strokes finishing in the lower zone will emphasize this particular zone. On the other hand, long and rising t-bars and high i-dots will give emphasis to the upper zone. A large-sized middle zone, especially if it is also very wide (sidewards emphasis), will give dominance to this zone. Where there are no other major extensions, the writer whose upper and lower zones are the same size and dominate equally will have an equal interest in both areas.

Some people accentuate various zones inappropriately, owing to psychological pressures. Anyone who frequently adds extra strokes to their upper and lower zones to make them longer and fuller is subconsciously adding to their self-confidence, because of feelings of anxiety. It is a neurotic sign, and is found in people who can cope with life only if they follow strict guidelines and do not deviate in any way from what they have decided is safe for them. They may also follow rituals, such as regular and frequent cleaning and checking doors and windows for security, and must have a regular schedule.

Remember that at this stage we are not looking at capital letters and signatures; they will be considered at a later stage.

The following tables show the attributes indicated by the different sizes of each zone.

Upper Zone High

Positive	Negative
Imaginative	Extravagant
Idealistic	Pretentious
Enthusiastic	Power-seeking
Ambitious	Lacking realism
Spiritually aware	Daydreaming

Upper Zone Low

Positive	Negative
Realistic	Lacking intellectual interests
Modest	Lacking spiritual awareness
Self-reliant	Lacking ambition

Middle Zone High

Positive	Negative
Desiring recognition	Very self-concerned
Self-assured	Subjective
Strongly emotional	Conceited
Interested in people	Desiring luxury

Middle Zone Low

Positive	Negative
Pays attention to detail	Petty and fussy
Modest	Pedantic
Contented	Lacking social interest
	Under tension
	Emotionally over-controlled

Lower Zone Long

Positive	Negative
Physically active	Clumsy (very heavy pressure)
Practical	Materialistic
Showing business acumen (light pressure)	
With strong sexual urges	

Lower Zone Short

Positive	Negative
Matter of fact	Sexually indifferent
Unmaterialistic	Physically weak (light pressure)

SLANT

Writing is an extroverted action; it is an attempt to share the writer's thoughts and feelings with others. The slant of the writing points to the degree of emotion and feeling the writer wishes to show, in the way of affectionate response to others. It is a bridge of communication from the writer to the reader.

Today the average slant is 80° – that is, 10° rightward of upright – as most people were taught. Before 1910 it was 60° and the writing was not so rounded, but there have been different variations throughout history. This is important to bear in mind if very old documents are being examined.

In the introduction I mentioned that a protractor would be useful to measure the slant accurately. For the purposes of an analysis, we classify slant as: very leftward, leftward, upright, rightward and very rightward. A small degree of variation, say 3° for upright, is to be expected – we are not machines.

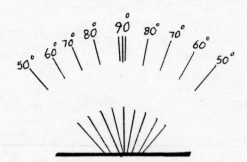

Look for any deviations and note where they occur. For example, if the last letter of a word which shows a rightward slant turns upright or leftwards, this indicates a tendency towards strong caution. The pressure may be heavier on this letter because of the slowing down process for the change in direction.

It must also be remembered that a left-handed person will automatically write with a leftward slant unless they turn the paper to the left to offset this and produce a rightward or upright slant. For the purpose of the personality assessment, however, the script should be considered as it is finally presented on the paper. I have usually found left-handed people persevering, enthusiastic and determined to get on in life.

Rightward slant

A rightward slant (see *figure 8*) indicates a willingness to share experiences with others, and these writers prefer to work in a group rather than by themselves. Basically they are extroverts; the extent of their extroversion depends upon the degree of the slant and the width (see 'Width' p.28). They will have many friends of the opposite sex, but many of these friendships, though affectionate, will be shallow. They need to express their devotion in an emotional way and will usually take the initiative in any outgoing enterprise or social activity.

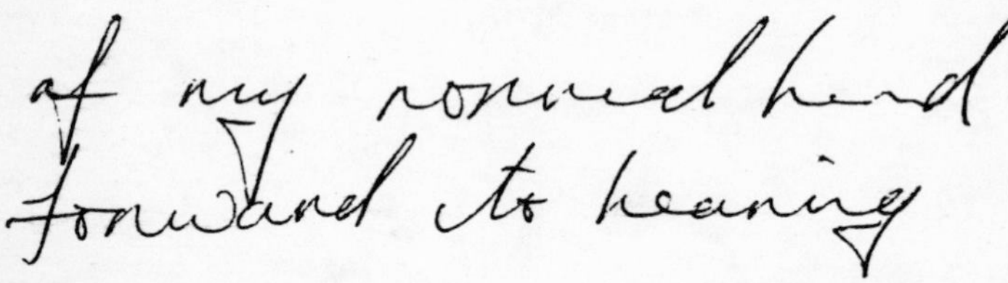

Figure 8

Extreme rightward slant (from 50 degrees downwards)

People with a very rightward slant are given to expressing excitement in an unrestrained way. They are very impatient and need to be mobile. It is not often that their judgement can be relied upon, because they are hasty in jumping to conclusions, without reasoning things through. They will also take a chance on things that others would consider calmly first. In the case of extremely rightward writing, of about 40°

slant, with the actual alignment irregular and the words almost illegible, the person will be highly strung and bordering on instability. Adolf Hitler wrote like this towards the end of his life.

Upright slant

With upright writing (see *figure 9*) the head rules the heart. Such writers are independent, cool, calm, collected, self-confident and objective. In very high Form Level writing, it indicates a business executive. These people are rarely excitable, and they are able to cope easily in an emergency. They prefer order and well-organized schedules, and work efficiently with others or by themselves. They are also adaptable and dependable, and they can be very detached in business, but sentimental at home if the writing is fairly rounded. In a relationship the upright writer is often accused of being aloof and uncaring, which is not quite correct. It is just their reserved manner which causes them to hide their emotions.

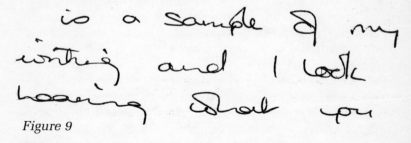

Figure 9

Leftward slant

The leftward slant (see *figure 10*) is the slant of the introvert and a very personal trait because no one has been taught to write in a leftward slant: it is therefore an isolation symbol.

Such people are usually defensive and ready to close themselves off from the world at large. They are more reserved than the upright writer and relate to past experiences rather than looking forward towards the future, of which they are often afraid. They are 'backroom' workers who are able and will actually prefer to work alone.

A leftward slant is more frequent in a female hand, but

when a male writes in a leftward direction he makes a good, sensitive partner, provided the other party is also a leftward writer. The reason for this is that unless there is an understanding between them, they will not be socially comfortable. If the male leftward writer also has small writing and fairly wide spacing between the words, he may also be petty and irritating in his mannerisms.

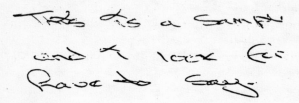

Figure 10

Extreme leftward slant

Very leftward writers with a fair to heavy pressure are awkward people who oppose everything they have not thought of themselves and reject others' attempts to befriend them. They are usually the product of an unhappy childhood.

A narrow, very leftward slant with heavy pressure, no loops in the upper or lower zones, pointed t-bars and angularly formed letters indicates someone unsympathetic, possibly aggressive, with anti-social, 'uptight' behaviour, who is difficult to live with. With the same indications, but a light pressure, the writer is less likely to be aggressive, but can still be awkward.

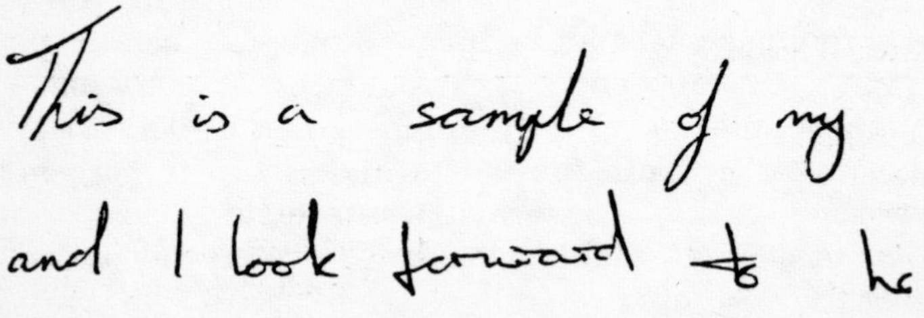

Figure 11

Mixed slant

There will be times when a Mixed Slant is found in an adult handwriting (see *figure 11*). These writers are torn between extrovert needs and introvert feelings. However, with a high to medium Form Level, they are versatile in their thinking. The inventor comes to mind, provided the mixed slant occurs in the upper zone, the intellectual sphere. However, his or her emotional response can be unpredictable – sometimes outgoing, sometimes withdrawn. Such writers can also be moody and will often change their minds in the midst of whatever they are doing.

The following tables summarize the characteristics of the different slants.

Right Slant

Positive (Normal rightward)	*Negative (Very rightward)*
Active	Unrestrained
Sympathetic	Excitable
Progressive	Tending towards hysteria
Emotional	Thoughtless
Relaxed	Susceptible to influence
Unselfish	Impatient
Forward-looking	Lacking control

Upright Slant

Positive	*Negative*
Reliable in an emergency	Unemotional
Self-sufficient	Unresponsive
Able to reason	Snobbish
Reserved	Self-centred
Level-headed	

Leftward Slant

Positive	*Negative*
Controlled	Pretentious
Determined	Withdrawn
Persistent	Obstinate
Tender-hearted	Fussy and pedantic
Self-protective	(particularly in a male)
Introspective	Malicious
Self-denying	Insecure

Mixed Slant

Positive	*Negative*
Mentally versatile when	Inconsistent
Form Level high	Changeable
	Moody
	Emotionally unstable

Counter-dominance

In relation to the basic slant, there will be times when you will find what is called 'counter-dominance'. This is a movement which is contrary to the dominant one. For instance, in a rightward slant, there may be some strong leftward movements, such as an i-dot or a t-bar ending leftwards, or a lower zone loop, as shown before. This would indicate that the general trend (rightward) is countered by the leftward movements, indicating that the inclination towards others and the outer world is not so strong as would at first appear. It can also happen in reverse: in a dominant leftward slant the end strokes could be rightward and long; so could the t-bars and i-dots, lessening the inhibition factor.

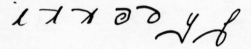

WIDTH

The width of each individual letter (not the spacing between the letters) is assessed as a variation from normal. The distance between the downstrokes is measured in relation to the height of the small letters, a, c, u, n, s etc, in the middle zone only. Take as an example the small letter 'n' – is it narrow or is it wide?

In regular writing, where the letters are even (see *chapter 5*), it will be constant; in an irregular script it will be varied (uneven), as will the other small letters.

    A wide script with a rightward slant confirms further the tendency towards an outgoing personality. *Figure 12* shows an example of a wide script.

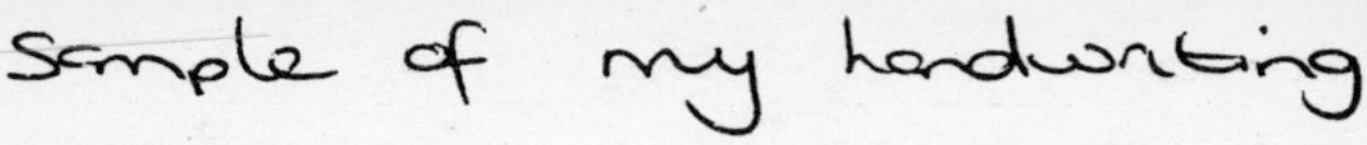

sample of my handwriting

Figure 12

Narrow letterforms with a rightward slant will point to a basically extrovert personality who is not so outgoing or spontaneous in expressing social ideas or mixing with others. The narrower the letters, the more cautious the writer will be, particularly in a leftward-slanted script, which you will remember indicates caution anyway. *Figure 13* shows an example of a narrow script.

sample of handwriting and I

Figure 13

An example of extreme narrowness is shown when the return downstroke covers the initial upstroke in the upper zone, and in the lower zone the initial downstroke is covered by the return stroke (see *figure 14*). These are *covering strokes* and indicate extreme inhibition. They also show a secretive nature. There will be no loops (for example, at the top of 'l's and the bottom of 'g's).

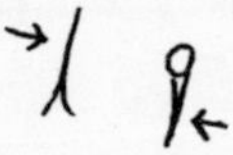

This depends upon which area of life is the dominant inhibitory factor, the intellectual or the sexual. For example, *figure 14* has covering strokes in both upper and lower zones. This writer is reluctant to reveal his or her plans and ideas (upper zone) as well as his or her sexual desires (lower zone).

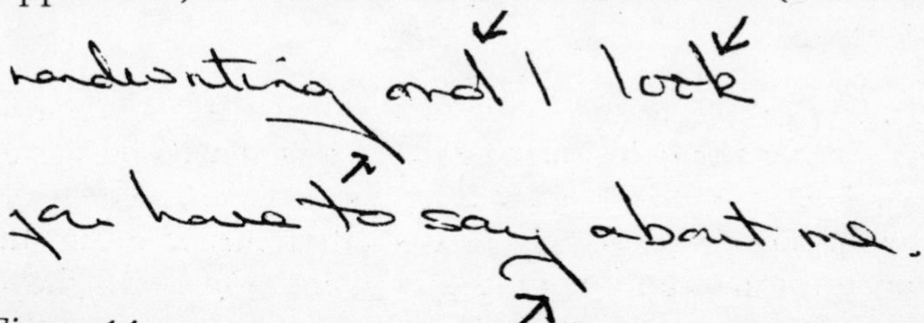

handwriting and I look

you have to say about me.

Figure 14

The following tables summarize the characteristics indicated by wide and narrow scripts.

Wide

Positive	Negative
Imaginative	Careless
Friendly	Hasty
Expressive	Extravagant
Sympathetic	Tending to lose control
Frank	Tactless
Outgoing	
Generous	

In addition to the above, a very wide script indicates someone who will avoid commitment if possible.

Narrow

Positive	Negative
Self-controlled	Critical
Reserved	Jealous
Economical with resources	Deceitful
	Distant
	Inhibited

In addition to the above, a very narrow script is indicative of secretiveness.

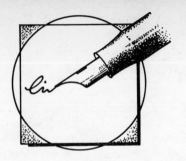

2 · LETTERS

CONNECTION AND FORM

Making the transition from printing to 'joined-up' writing is a big and important step for schoolchildren and the extent and form of a writer's connecting strokes will tell us a great deal about him or her.

Connected writing is writing in which four or more letters are connected together in a fluent movement (see *figure 15*). Breaks after punctuation or capitals are not counted, and do not affect our assessment of connection.

Figure 15

DEGREE OF CONNECTION

Connected writing indicates that the writer is a logical thinker who prefers to work in a systematic way. He or she is also co-operative and sociable.

Occasionally one finds in otherwise connected writing breaks which are syllabic. The writer thinks in terms of syllables and breaks the train of thought in this way, spelling by hearing the words in his or her mind. There are also writers who break for t-bars and i-dots, while others continue writing, then go back to insert them. Others connect the i-dot or t-bar to the next letter – a sign of an agile mind. All these styles are regarded as connected writing. Some writers connect not only the letters but also some of the words. This is known as *extreme connection* (see *figure 16*). These writers usually connect in a specific zone, normally the upper or middle zones only. This factor is associated with over-fatigue, as if the writer is driving him or herself to complete a job and refuses to allow anything to interrupt the flow. Such people can be over-anxious and tense.

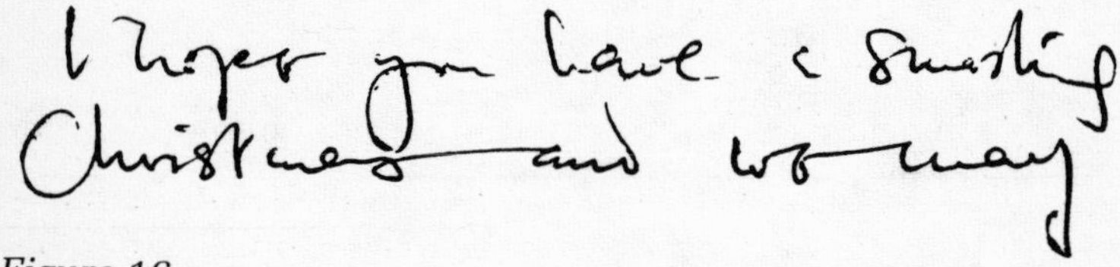

Figure 16

Disconnected writing (see *figure 17*) occurs when no more than three letters are connected at a time. The positive aspect of disconnected writers is intuitive thinking, the negative aspect a lack of co-ordinated concentration ('grasshopper' thinking). They are inclined to be more individual in their likes and dislikes and are less co-operative or socially minded than connected writers. They work easily alone and keep their own counsel. They often suffer from loneliness (if there is wide spacing between the words and lines), but would not admit it to anyone. They can also be more nervous and spasmodic than connected writers. You will occasionally find that writers who are very anxious and compulsive in their habits will make amendments to their letters and other corrections to their writing to make it look better – or so they think. In fact they often make it illegible.

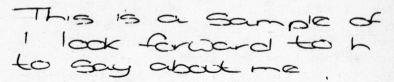

Figure 17

Many disconnected writers, particularly when the forms are original (see 'Letterforms', p.40), are artistic and inventive, as their intuitive minds dictate individuality.

Very wide unexplained gaps between letters within a word indicate serious nervous tension, with lapses in concentration and memory; this could indicate a potential nervous breakdown. The writer should be warned to be less intense and advised to visit a doctor.

It will be found that many styles of handwriting are both connected and disconnected, with neither clearly dominant. These writers are adaptable to circumstances. When the writing is also irregular, with weak pressure, they will be emotionally sensitive (see *figure 18*). They are people with good ideas, but they can be impatient and irritated by trivia and what they consider to be irrelevant issues.

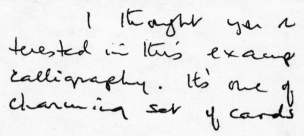

Figure 18

Let us now summarize the characteristics of the two degrees of connection.

Connected

Positive	*Negative*
Logical	Fatigued (in the case of
Sociable	extreme connection)
Purposeful	Impulsive (if very fast)
Co-operative	
Systematic	
Consistent	

Disconnected

Positive	*Negative*
Adaptable	Lacking versatility
Full of ideas	Inconsistent
Inventive	Lacking forethought
Independent	
Intuitive	
Individualistic	

FORM OF CONNECTION

The various forms of connection are, in fact, developments and deviations from the copybook, the first form of letters learned during early school days (see *figure 19*).

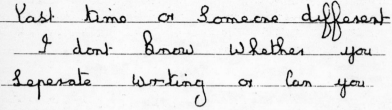

Figure 19

For reasons of ease or expediency, depending on personality, some people do not vary much from their first learned form of writing. These writers have very little cause to write and no incentive to expand their minds once they have left school. They find their security by adhering to what they think is expected of them; their experience is therefore limited. It must be emphasized that for this description to apply all three zones should be consistent with copybook style in the form of connection, each one being no different from the others.

The age of the writer will also be relevant. If the person is over 70 years of age, he or she was probably taught an angular form of connection (see *figure 20*) and if there is no change, it is to be assumed that he or she appreciates the restriction and discipline. The same applies to someone who adopts the Italic style in adult life; such a person will be conscious of the aesthetic form and therefore artistically aware.

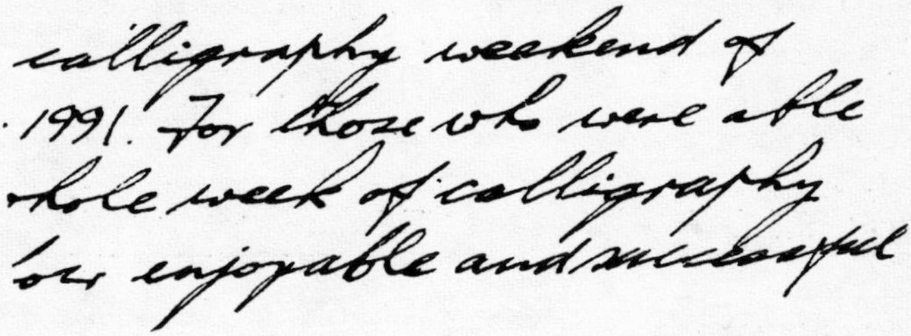

Figure 20

In disconnected writing, it may be difficult to establish what form of connection is being used, because of the lack of connecting strokes. It is helpful to examine the small letter 'm' in this respect. Moreover a slow writing speed (see *chapter 6*) will suggest that the form of connection is copybook, arcade (see *figure 21*) or angular.

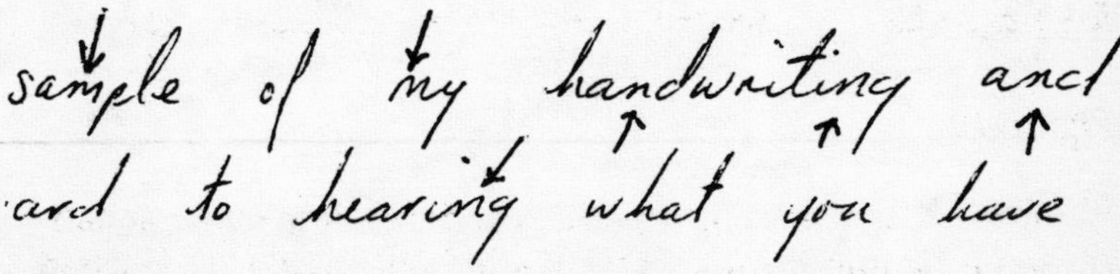

Figure 21

Garland (see *figure 22*), where the letters 'm' and 'n' resemble the letters 'w' and 'u', is usually the result of connected fast writing, as are the wavy line (see *figure 23*) and thread (see *figure 24*) forms. These forms are not taught initially in school; they are the result of connected, fast writing developing as a personal style later.

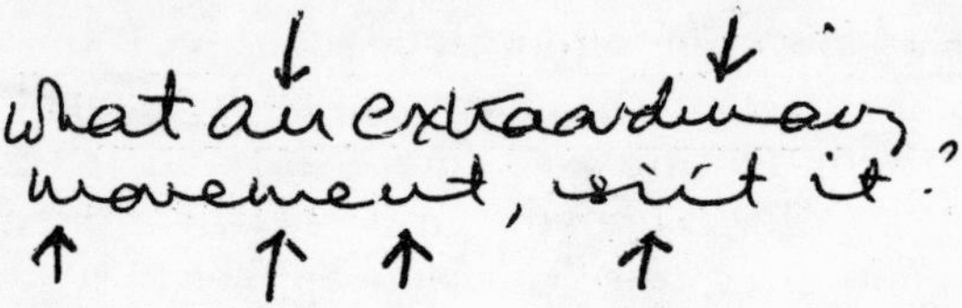

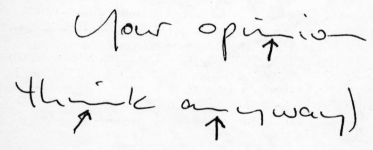

Figure 22

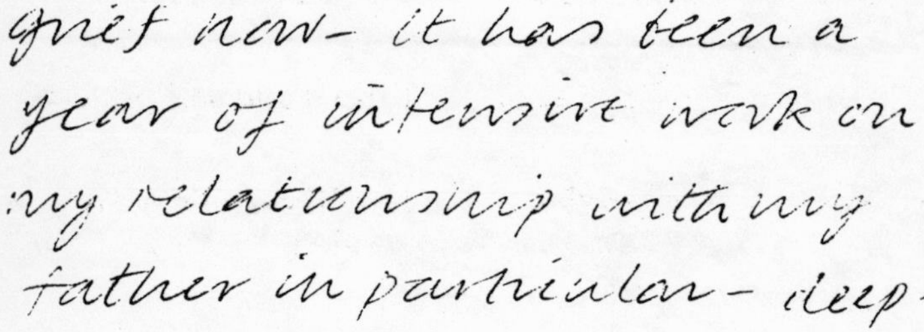

grief now— it has been a
year of intensive work on
my relationship with my
father in particular — deep—

Figure 23

Your opinion

think anyway)

Figure 24

There are often two forms of connection in the same writing. The dominant one can usually be found by careful examination, and the second form is only subsidiary. The dominant one is the overriding factor and the subsidiary one indicates secondary features in terms of personality. Both should be included in the final assessment.

Examples of Forms of Connection

Forms		Basic Indication
COPYBOOK	*muin*	Conventional
(Curved at the top and bottom)		
GARLAND	*uuuu*	Open and responsive
ARCADE	*mmm*	Closed and self-protective
ANGULAR	*wwww*	Needing challenge or conflict
WAVY LINE	*nnn*	Avoiding of conflict
THREAD	*~~~*	Gliding through life, taking the easy way out

The garland connection is open to additions and elaborations; thus angular garland is not unusual. This can be thought of as the 'iron fist in the velvet glove' approach – the garland complies and the angle resists.

The main indications of each form of connection are as follows.

Copybook

Positive	Negative
Orthodox	Lacking initiative
Predictable	Lacking originality

It is possible that, for professional reasons, a person such as a teacher or a nurse may need to write slowly and clearly, as in a copybook style. In the case of a nun or a priest, copybook could indicate humility.

Garland

Positive	Negative
Sincere	Submissive
Very adaptable	Under-challenged
Avoiding argument	Lazy
Affectionate and warm	Changeable
Tolerant	
Very socially minded	

Arcade

Positive	Negative
Very reserved	Critical
Formal	Morally repressed
Independent	With a closed mind
Traditional	Inflexible
Constructive and practical	

Angle

Positive	Negative
Conventional	Unadaptable
Stable	Quarrelsome
Ethical	Unsympathetic
Logical	Rigid
Determined	Domineering
Mentally agile	

Wavy Line

Positive	*Negative*
Diplomatic	Prone to changing
Keen to preserve individuality	direction under pressure
Subjective	Following the general trend
	Avoiding commitments if
	possible

Thread

Positive (medium to strong pressure)	*Negative (light pressure)*
Wanting freedom to follow	Indefinite and ambiguous
creative talent	Avoiding troublesome
Reluctant to be tied down to	issues
convention	Manipulative
Inclined to act according to	Sometimes excitable
own instincts	Lacking self-assurance
Opposed to any form of	Inclined to nervous
aggression	disturbances (look for
Willing to adopt new attitudes	small middle zone)
for self-protection and to	Unable to withstand
preserve individuality	stressful pressures
Strong in empathy	Unwilling to make or
Possessing a psychological	adhere to commitments
insight into others	Anti authority
	Lacking a sense of
	obligation

Thread at the end of a word, as in '-ing' (see *figure 25*), is less significant than thread within a word, which points to a person who is not averse to lying, or who is being economical with the truth.

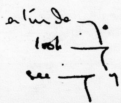

Figure 25

LETTERFORMS

Psychologically, the more people emphasize the external impression of their work – how it looks – the more concerned they are with the extravagant aspects of their performance, and this can be seen in the degree of ornamentation in a sample of writing. At its worst the overloading of the letters will disturb the basic rhythm and will look rather strange. At its best there will be a satisfying balance between the rhythmic harmony, the writer's individuality and the essential form of the letters. Intelligent, productive people know what to put in and what to leave out. This is closely related to Form Level – that is, the overall quality of the writing (see *chapter 6*). Ornamentation is negative because it is unnecessary and wastes time and effort.

Copybook writing has been discussed under 'Form of Connection' above, and the letterforms are shown in *figure 19*. The other types of letterform are as follows.

Simplified

This is a deviation from copybook, with strokes reduced to a bare minimum while maintaining legibility (see *figure 26*). It is usually found in a high Form Level.

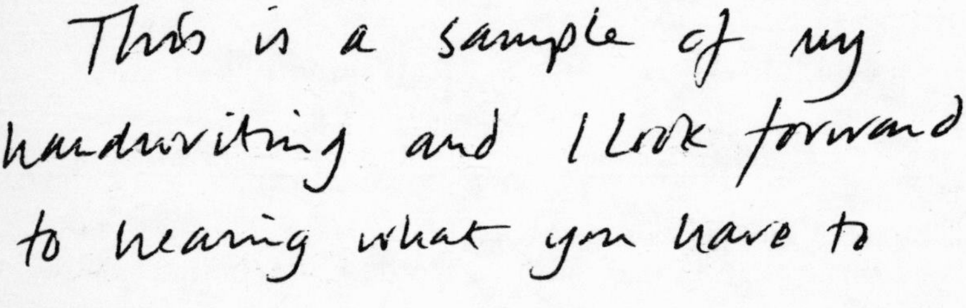

This is a sample of my handwriting and I look forward to hearing what you have to

Figure 26

It indicates a practised writer with no time for overworked, stylistic or fanciful forms, who has an active mind and intellectual interests and is aware of what is, and what is not, essential.

Neglected

Even the bare essentials are omitted in this form (see *figure 27*), making the writing difficult to read.

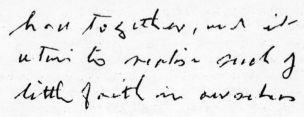

Figure 27

These people will cut corners and evade the issue whenever possible if the matter is unimportant to them. They dislike anything which demands concentration; they find it tedious within a short time. However, they usually have lively minds and respond intelligently to subjects with which they are personally involved in order to remain interested.

Complicated and enriched

Here, the writing, whilst having an individual style with individual forms, is legible (see *figure 28*). To fall into this category, therefore, the elaboration must be in good taste and artistic.

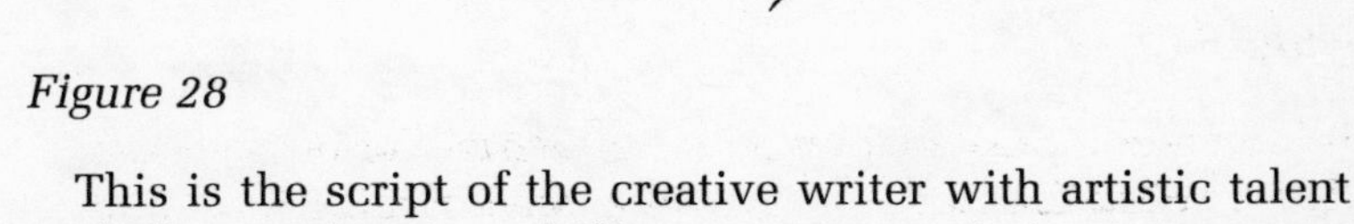

Figure 28

This is the script of the creative writer with artistic talent and the productive ability to express it in some way. Whatever such a person undertakes will have a pleasing degree of presentation.

Overloaded and artificially flourished

The writing shown in *figure 29* is always a product of a low
Form Level writer. Every word is overshadowed by superfluous strokes and additions which destroy the clarity. The
writing, in fact, looks vulgar.

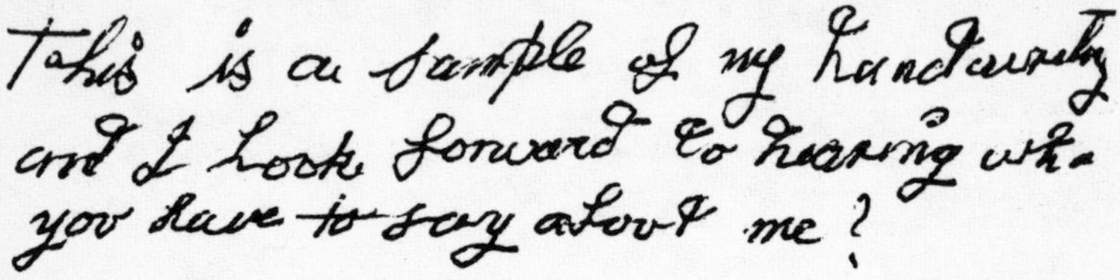

Figure 29

Such writers are vain and conceited, needing to be accept-
ed by others as 'nice people'. This need is normally a compensation for feelings of inferiority. They lack objectivity and
good taste and make unreliable workers because they are
constantly looking for support from superiors, and feeling
rejected if it is not given; this may ultimately lead to more
ostentatious behaviour to gain attention. They see their crude
and ornamental script as calligraphic, which it is not.

If you are examining an early English script, however,
remember that the Copperplate style was prescribed by the
copybooks of that time, which stipulated flourishes (see *figure 30*).

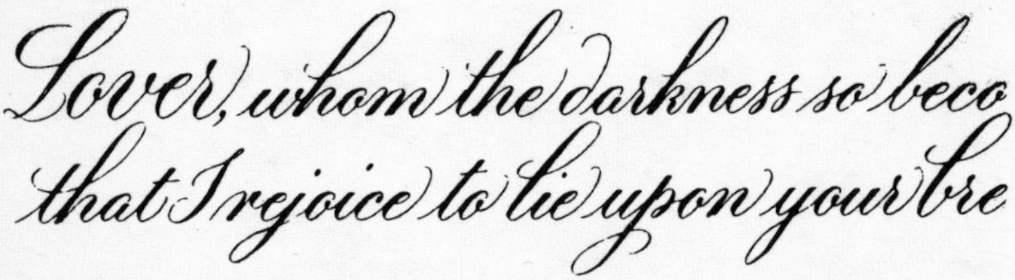

Figure 30

The main indications of the different types of letterform
are as follows.

Simplified	Neglected
Positive	*Negative*
Reliable judgement	Unreliable
Intellectual	Slapdash attitude
Objective	Inconsiderate
Natural behaviour pattern	Lack of precision
Mature attitude	Undecisive
Clear thinking ability	Unpunctual
Aesthetic awareness	Ambiguous ideas
Purposeful	

Complicated and Enriched	Overloaded with ornament
Positive	*Negative*
Creative	Vain
Dignified	Pompous
Original	Conceited
Aesthetic tastes	Poor taste
Flexible ideas	Insincere
Practical versatility	

3 · Pen Strokes

We'll now go on to look at some more subtle features of handwriting, examining the effect of 'shading' (thickness and thinness of strokes) and differences in pressure.

DESCRIPTION OF THE STROKE

Early graphologists were more fortunate in some ways than we are today, because people took great care in choosing a pen that gave them personal satisfaction in producing a particular type of thick and thin stroke. Nowadays they tend to use any pen that comes to hand – often a ballpoint – except professional people, who still tend to use fountain pens for important letters.

The three dominant types of stroke you will encounter are *sharp*, *distinct* and *pastose*.

Sharp

This is a thin stroke with normal pressure, and there is no differentiation between the up and down strokes (see *figure 31*). The ends of the words or, in disconnected writing, the ends of the letters, will have sharp points, particularly the t-bars.

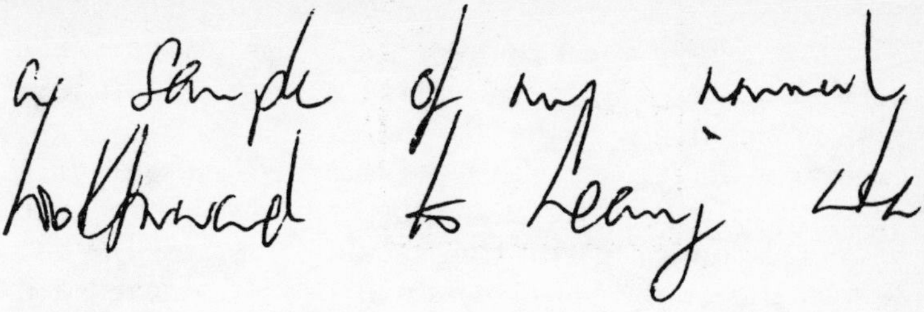

Figure 31

Sharp writers lack sensitivity and can be emotionally very cold. They freely criticize things with which they do not agree (particularly if their writing is angular). They have great self-discipline and a strong determination. They depend upon their principles and can also be pedantically awkward in wanting their own way. Resentment can follow any rejection of their ideas and ideals, which will have been well thought out. Where the t-bar is particularly long and sharp (like a javelin) their criticism will be expressed verbally, with little restraint. The sharp writer has a penetrating mind and will follow intellectual pursuits and subjects; the higher the Form Level (see *chapter 6*), the more this will apply. Such people have difficulty in enjoying life to the full because of their need to criticize. In spite of this they are themselves sometimes emotionally vulnerable, although they will never admit it, unless forced to do so.

Distinct (shaded)
This stroke has a distinction between the up and down strokes (see *figure 32*).

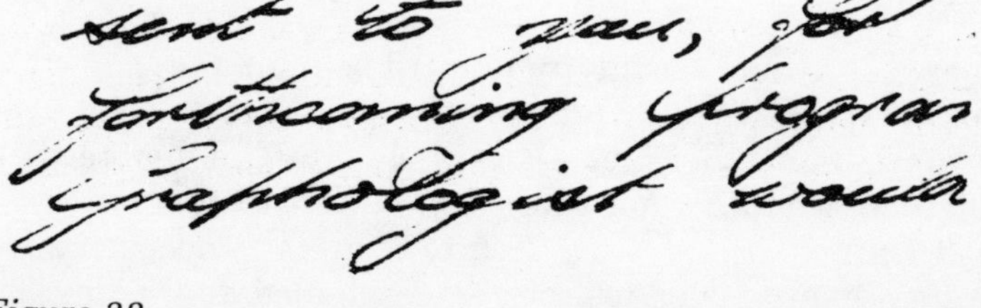

Figure 32

The critical discernment in this case is usually creative. This stroke, which is less common nowadays, does not lend itself to quick writing, indicating a less spontaneous response compared with the sharp stroke. There is normally a respect for traditional values and a reliable sense of duty. These writers will sacrifice comfort if necessary and will place correctness high on their scale of values. Usually angles, small size and narrowness will also be evident. Their attitude to life is serious. They may be reliable workers, provided they can set their own moderate pace. They will resent being pushed into action.

Pastose
Think of the ink being squeezed out of a tube and put on with a brush, with no distinction between the up and down strokes: the immediate impression is that of thick writing, which it is (see *figure 33*). This is the result of the pen being held at a more slanting angle, so that there is more nib on the surface of the paper and therefore more ink. When writing with a ballpoint pen, these writers prefer a thicker one. They also like a thick paper on which to write.

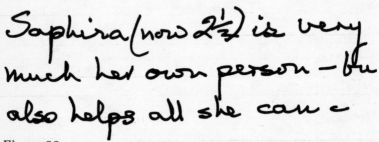

Figure 33

There is a strong sensitivity to tactile stimulation and such people are dominated by their senses. These must be brought into play in any social or pleasurable situation before they can experience fully their desires and needs, particularly in a sexual context where warm bodily contact is necessary for their dominant sensual feelings to be satisfied. In this respect the imagination can be intense. Ideally, their partners should be amenable to their warm, emotional 'hands-on' contact, and therefore should preferably not be a sharp-stroke writer, who might object to this intense closeness.

They are very sentimental, as will usually be evident in their personality expression. They have a preference for strong colours and the visual arts and will usually have developed a sense of beauty (look for originality in the script). They can be easily led by a sensual person of the opposite sex. They have a heightened sense of touch, smell, taste and visual contact.

On the negative side, they can lack self-discipline, indulge in daydreaming, have little moral discrimination and lack ambition and restraint.

Look out also for filled-in loops; these writers are full of anxiety over minor problems. Where the script has a smeary look, particularly with heavy t-bars, and the writing is slow, it is a sign of brutality and outbursts of temper. Such people can also be undisciplined in seeking sexual pleasures, and resort to alcohol where there is no outlet for these desires to be fulfilled.

The following is a summary of the characteristics of the strokes discussed here.

Sharp

Positive	Negative
Analytically minded	Lacking sensuality
Self-disciplined	Resentful
Spiritually aware	Emotionally cold
Determined	Quarrelsome
Possessing a penetrating mind	Critical and argumentative

Distinct

Positive	Negative
Artistically aware	Slow
Possessing a good sense of duty	Pedantic

Pastose

Positive	*Negative*
Emotionally warm	Materialistic
Sensual	Crude
Possessing good colour sense	Lacking spirituality
Able to absorb tension	Self-indulgent
Possessing a strong sexual imagination	Lazy

PRESSURE

It is important to understand the significance of the pressure pattern in any analysis of handwriting.

First the writing paper should be considered. If it is very thick, more pressure will be needed to maintain a progressive movement outwards towards the right-hand side, even for a left-handed writer. If the paper is very thin, then less pressure is exerted to avoid tearing, particularly if a ballpoint pen which gives a thin stroke is used. In my experience, the heavy-pressure writer usually prefers a thick ballpoint pen or a broad nib. Of course it is always possible that the writer has no say in the choice of paper which may be company stationery, usually of good quality and thick.

Note that the line produced by a felt-tip pen may give the impression of heavy pressure having been used, when this is not necessarily so. If you have the original document (and you should not work on photocopies until you are experienced), turn the paper over and look at the indentation: this is a guide to the amount of force used. Through the interplay of muscular contraction and release, the force will depend upon the vitality and the mood of the writer at the time of writing – an angry person, for example, will apply more force. Moreover, a slow writer, who uses a pen only occasionally, will produce more depth than someone who writes frequently, and who will move forward faster. The pressure will therefore be heavier.

A slow writer is also likely to be writing a copybook form, perhaps because he or she is not accustomed to writing. The more intellectual writer will be using the angular or arcade form, which is faster than copybook, and where the pressure pattern should be centred upon the down strokes. An arcade writer is usually not as fast as a garland writer, and the pressure will be medium to heavy. The garland writer will usually be using a lighter pressure because of the faster speed at which the garland movement is formed, the flow being smoother.

The script of a medium-pressure writer has very little to offer in the way of personality and character assessment. You should therefore note 'normal' on your worksheet and move on to the other features.

You should not accept a pencil script until you have gained a great deal of experience, since the various hard to soft grades can be confusing.

Light pressure

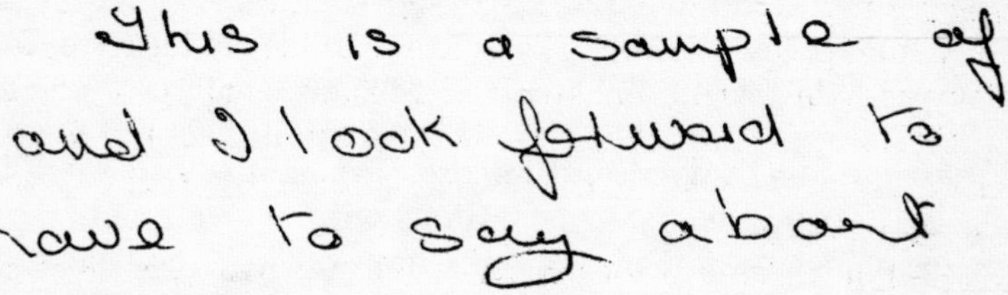

Figure 34

Light pressure is a feminine sign (see *figure 34*), and people who write in this way are sensitive, usually cultured and well mannered. Their psychic energy is used in their work or leisure interests, where they are economical with their physical resources. They are mentally agile, receptive, adaptable and modest. They pace their efforts with a delicacy of feeling, and at the end of their day they are less tired than the heavy-pressure writers, who are inclined to wear themselves out in irrelevant actions. Light-pressure people avoid conflict if possible; their persistence and willpower is less intense than that of heavy-pressure writers. Nor would they boast of physical prowess in any sporting activity.

Heavy pressure

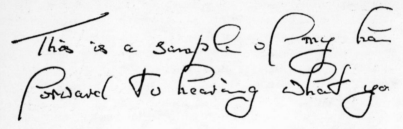

Figure 35

Heavy pressure is a masculine sign (see *figure 35*), and these writers are motivated by energetic pursuits. They tend to overstretch themselves in their determination to get things moving and are tenacious in achieving their aims. They often cannot adapt quickly to new routines and may refuse to be receptive to other people's ideas. This is particularly true of angular writers, who often lack consideration.

Emotional experiences are not as deeply absorbed as in light-pressure writers who can be easily hurt. Heavy-pressure writers usually like plenty of activity and prefer to be kept fully occupied in work and leisure. This could lead them to take on too much and frustration could occur when their achievements do not match their hopes. They then become casualties of stress and strain.

Very heavy pressure on the down strokes (see *figure 36*) is directed towards the writer, whereas heavy pressure on the sideward (rightward) strokes is directed towards others and the environment. Incidentally, a club-like, heavy-pressured t-bar points to a very aggressive person who can resort to violence. The writing will be irregular and the Form Level, through lack of intellect, will be low in this instance.

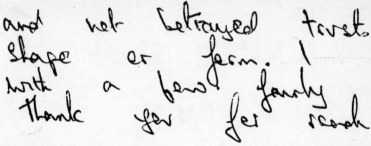

Figure 36

Variable pressure

You may find that the pressure pattern you are examining is both light and heavy – variable and disturbed (see *figure 37*).

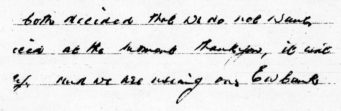

Figure 37

This is not a good sign. It indicates emotional imbalance, an indecisive thought process and probable feelings of inferiority that are not being addressed in a useful way, resulting in anxiety of a neurotic nature.

The following is a summary of the characteristics of the different pressure patterns.

Light Pressure

Positive	Negative
Adaptable	Superficial
Modest	Timid
Feminine	Low in energy reserves
Sensitive	Lacking resistance
Mentally agile	Lacking initiative

Heavy Pressure

Positive	Negative
Possessing strong willpower	Aggressive
Possessing reserves of vitality	Clumsy
Warm emotionally	Obstinate
Self-controlled	Vain
Seeking success	Excitable

Varied Pressure (disturbed)

	Negative
	Indecisive
	Unreliable in mood
	With personality disturbances
	Unpredictable
	Irritable
	Experiencing alcohol problems

INITIAL AND TERMINAL STROKES

We will now consider the initial and terminal strokes all adult writers make as they begin and finish a word. These strokes indicate whether or not one needs to prepare oneself before going into action, even when only writing one word, and whether one is able to control one's thinking once it is in motion.

Where there are no initial strokes apart from those that are a functional part of the letter, the writer is spontaneously motivated without undue deliberation, and will be direct in his or her approach. The faster the writing speed the more constructive he or she will be towards the task in hand; mental preparation and excessive concern with detail will be unnecessary.

Where there are long initial strokes (see *figure 38*), the writer has a tendency to waste time and effort before going ahead, particularly when the writing is unhurried and the thought process is slow to comprehend what is required.

They also indicate a lack of self-assurance. There can also be a positive indication, however: a long initial stroke before the first letter of a word in fast writing acts as a springboard to action. There is no stopping these writers once they get going (see *figure 38*).

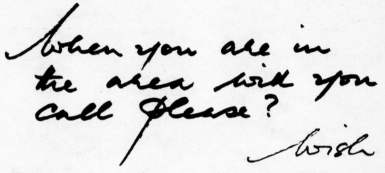

Figure 38

The terminal or end strokes may be normal, curtailed or extended as a dominant feature and this factor is associated with the writer's outgoing inclination – it reaches out to others, curves in towards the self or is just anti-social.

The ideal letter to examine for the terminal stroke is the small letter 'd' or 'e'.

de   Normal disposition, conventional

e   May be suspicious of others' motives

d e   Selfish attitude; anti-social; reticent; resistant to change; abrupt manner

e   Always daydreaming; could be excessively religious

e   Physically aggressive; resentful; bad-tempered

Always relating to the past; self-protective; interested primarily in self; very cautious

Wants his or her own way; awkward attitude

Small letter 'e' like 'i', closed in fast writing, with a covering stroke. Quick in comprehension; secretive; inhibited

Enjoys cultured pursuits, literary interests

These strokes should be considered only at the word ending, not where they are connected to the next letter.

Long terminal strokes that end with a small hook or a tick show persistence and tenacity. The writer may also take a defensive attitude. A graceful terminal with a fairly short stroke that rises towards the next word indicates a generous nature.

Any end stroke that finishes leftward indicates a tendency towards self-interest.

The opposite denotes a person who starts with a spontaneity which is curbed as each line is completed. Such individuals will show an enthusiastic initial response, then retreat rather than commit themselves further:

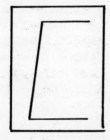

Irregularity in the right-hand margin is to be expected to a certain degree, but most people will organize their writing to give a natural effect of evenness – planning will avoid the cramming in of a word.

An excessively wide right-hand margin may mean the person is afraid to approach life and has great problems in coping with personal issues. This is often seen in suicide letters, where the spacing of the words is also abnormally wide:

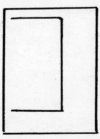

The upper margin is related to planning ability and foresight. There should be a comfortable space allowed for the address and date. If it is too narrow, it is indicative of a person who will not respect another's privacy. It also could mean a lack of education, in which case there will be poor Form Level. Too wide a top margin points to a snobbish, vain and pretentious writer (look also for large capital letters).

The lower margin should have a reasonable space for the signature and not be cramped; again planning and foresight is called for in visualizing the length of the letter in order to leave the correct amount of space. There should not be writing round the side margins. This is usually the sign of a child-like writer (in which case there could also be small pictures) or a very miserly individual.

It is, of course, always essential to examine other factors before committing oneself to a final opinion on the basis of margins.

THE ENVELOPE

The envelope should be assessed in the same way as the margins. Is the address too far to the left or right, too near to the stamp and franking area (as is often the case with children), or cramped along the bottom? Bear in mind also that the address on an envelope should be completely legible.

The usual indications of the three zones and left and right also apply to the envelope: writing on the upper part indicates daydreaming and on the lower part the need for material possessions; writing towards the left indicates a preference for the past and towards the right an orientation to the future and other people.

Excessive underlining on the envelope is the work of a pedantic and fussy individual who lacks common sense. It is frequently found when the envelope is 'overdone' – often amended – and in heavy-pressured writing.

DISTANCE BETWEEN WORDS

The personal spacing of each writer is not easily varied for long, even by conscious effort. We write as we speak, slowly, moderately or quickly, and space our words accordingly. In fact speech and writing are very closely related.

The average writer will space his or her words at between one and one and a half times the normal letter width – neither too crowded nor too far apart. What we are looking for as graphologists is the same as with other features: the deviation from the normal copybook recommendation. The spacing of the words will be assessed as normal, very narrow, very wide or very irregular.

A good organizer will space his or her words normally, showing an orderliness of thinking and good factual presentation resulting from good judgement and power of observation (see *figure 39*).

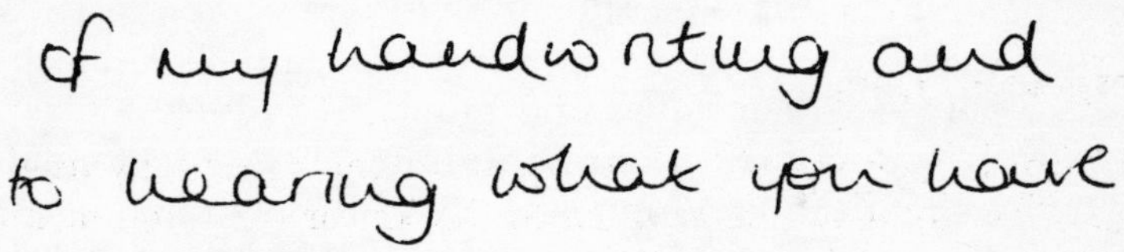

of my handwriting and
to hearing what you have

Figure 39

Words that are crowded together point to a talkative person who has a compulsive need for other people and fears isolation. These writers can be obtrusive and tactless but are usually warm-hearted and moderately generous.

When the script is also very irregular the writer is impatient to keep mobile and active, often becoming anxious without a valid reason. Such people function by instinct – the area of the unconscious, with a normal to long lower zone – rather than by reasoning, and their judgement can be rather subjective. They rely on their emotional feelings and this is usually right for them (see *figure 40*).

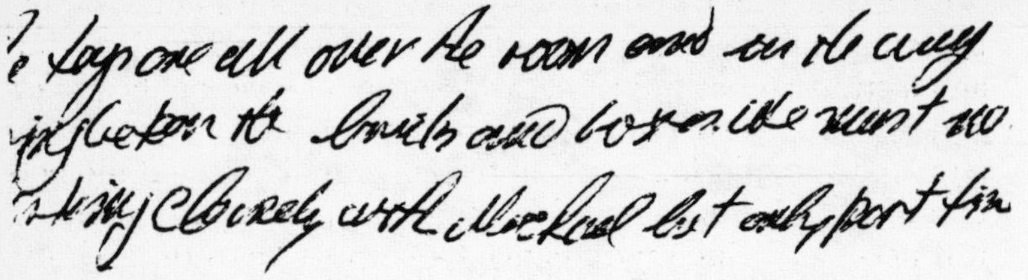

Figure 40

When the spacing between the words is very wide, it is a sign of isolation and reserve beyond what is normal. These writers are very cautious about friendship and, because they can be critical of others, they could mistakenly be considered inconsiderate and unsociable.

Writers with very wide spacing are often compensating for a hurtful experience, usually with the opposite sex, or even with parents. They are emotionally withdrawn and fear that if they try to form a friendship they will fail. They erect a barrier between themselves and others to avoid the disappointment which a rejection would bring. They are therefore bringing about the very opposite of what they really want, which is a close, emotional personal involvement. The greater their solitude, the wider the distance between the words – and also the lines, which we will now consider.

DISTANCE BETWEEN LINES

The distance between lines should, of course, be assessed on plain, unlined paper. The underlengths of the lower zone should just clear the upper zone of the following line. If there are any exaggerations in either zone there will have to be an adjustment, which will affect the horizontal spacing as the writer has to move forward to avoid mingling, or else increase the distance between the lines to maintain clarity. If the only sample you have is written on lined paper, check whether there is a tendency to write above or below the printed lines: this suggests that there would be variations if the paper were plain.

Clear line spacing indicates a clear mind with constructive thinking and discerning faculties, a good sense of direction and a strong sense of justice. Exactly equal spacing, however, could be the result of a guide inserted beneath the writing paper and rigidly followed. In this case, look to see if the bottom of the middle zone follows the line, putting a ruler along it if necessary. Such writers need a helping hand through the pressures of daily life.

If the lines are far apart and the word spacing is also very wide, the writer needs urgent help in coming to terms with loneliness and feelings of isolation. It is, in fact, one of the signs of suicide, in which case look also for a very wide right-hand margin and a very small and contracted or crossed-out signature, a sign of the rejection of the Ego, the inner self.

Mingling lines (see *figure 41*) are a sign of muddleheadedness and poor organization.

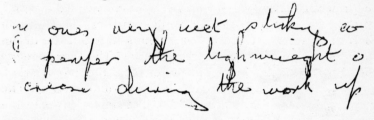

Figure 41

It is likely that this writer's Form Level will be low. The higher Form Level writer will adjust the spacing to avoid the upper zone of the current line mingling with the lower zone of the line above (see *figure 42*).

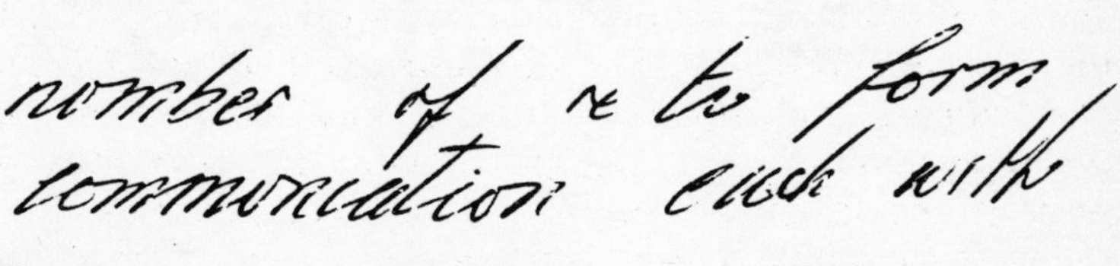

Figure 42

Such writers are careful workers and considerate to others. Remember, however, that the high upper zone can indicate a strong imagination and, where there are also wide loops, daydreaming. High loops are not so easily arranged to avoid mingling, unless the lines are very widely spaced (see *figure 43*). Daydreamers are usually slow in thinking and action.

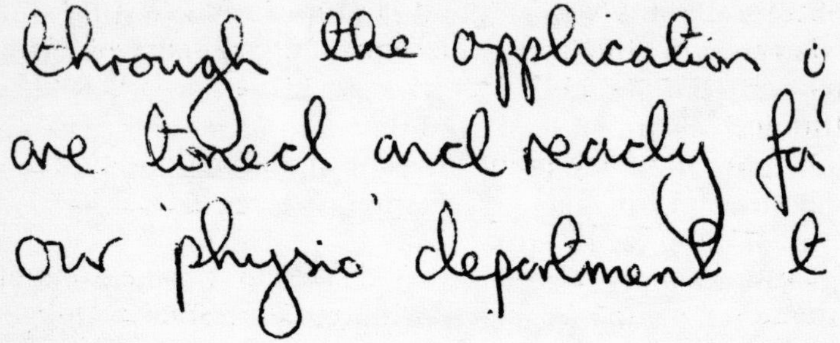

Figure 43

Most of the writing you will see will have clear line spacing, with just a slight variation on the occasional line (see *figure 44*). This is normal, and indicates a clear, uncluttered mind.

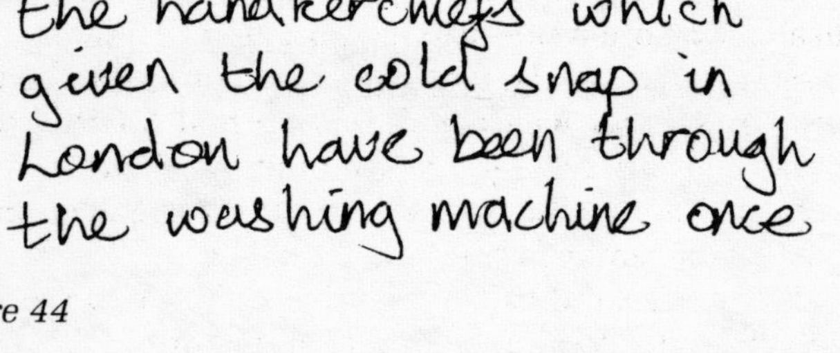

Figure 44

LINE DIRECTION

Ideally the lines of writing should be horizontal within 2°
rise or fall:

Straight lines with a good rhythm indicate a reliable,
orderly and methodical writer with good self-control. With a
rigid rhythm the individual would be rather inflexible in
attitude.

A rising line may point to optimism, ambition and initiative:

However, if the rise is extreme the writer may be excitable,
in which case the script will be irregular. Such people are
usually restless and need to keep mobile:

Lines that descend indicate tiredness, which can cause the
arm to move towards the body rather than outwards, and
points also to anxiety and depression – usually temporary –
so great care is needed. A pessimistic attitude can also cause
a falling line:

If it is known that the writer is old then a shaky stroke
quality may be evident. An arthritic hand or other evidence
of ill health will often produce a falling line.

In cases of extreme rise or fall, further samples should be
obtained to confirm whether this is normal for this writer.
Where the lines are regularly spaced but are rising or falling,
the effect may be the result of the paper having been held at
an angle; again, care is needed.

Undulating lines indicate a sensitive writer of nervous disposition, lacking a certain amount of self-control:

When accompanied by a thready script in a high Form
Level, it signifies versatility, and in a low Form Level un-

reliability of some kind – probably poor time-keeping or constant changes of mind, or both! This is also one of the signs for dishonesty, but be warned: not less than five indications are necessary to make such an assessment valid.

Occasionally, you will find that a line of writing is straight until very near to the right margin, where it falls:

This suggests lack of planning.

Lines that begin by rising, then fall, indicate that the writer begins enthusiastically but lacks the initiative or interest to carry on and is easily bored:

A line which falls at the beginning, then rises to the end, indicates that the writer suffers from self-doubt, but quickly recovers and is a good finisher in spite of his initial reluctance or tiredness:

Not only may the lines rise or fall, but so may the words. This is called *tiling*. Each word may start low on the base line and rise throughout the whole line of writing:

The initial enthusiasm or emotional response is continually being curbed.

Conversely the words may start high and fall:

This indicates that the writer is fighting discouragement or fatigue. In the case of acute fatigue, the pressure could also be disturbed, from moderately light to very light. If the problem is psychological, for instance worry and depression, the pressure disturbance will range from moderately heavy to very heavy. An unconscious adjustment will be taking place according to the compensatory needs of the writer.

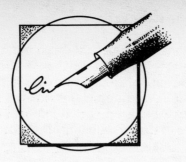

5 · REGULARITY AND RHYTHM

A vital part of the personality of handwriting is contributed by the two features we examine in this chapter. We'll look at the degree of uniformity (or otherwise) in a writer's letters and we'll also begin to analyse the very distinct 'flow' or rhythm of a writer's script.

REGULARITY

Normal writing is not too rigid nor too haphazard in height and direction. Because humans are not machines, there should also be a degree of variation in the script of a mature adult. Generally, regular writing indicates an emotionally balanced individual, not too staid nor too excitable.

But what should you look for in order to assess the degree of regularity? It is vital that you get it right, so take your time and consider each factor carefully. Later, when you are more experienced, you will quickly observe the regularity factor and remember what it means in terms of emotional response.

You should examine:

- **The height of the small letters** (the writer's attitude to daily life and routine). Are the letters of regular height, or irregular, and to what degree – slight to very uneven?

- **The variation of the slant** (willingness to share, self-reliance, introversion/extroversion). Is the slant consistently in one direction only – leftward, upright or rightward – or does it vary? Does this apply in all zones or just one?
- **The distance between the down strokes of the letters** (sharing, restraint or freedom in terms of progress). Are they even or uneven in distance, depending upon the letter shape?
- **The distance between the lines of writing** – unlined paper only (mental organization – tidy or confused mind). This is usually the factor that is most regular.

Regular

You will find that most of your handwriting samples are fairly regular, bearing in mind the natural variations which we all have in our writing.

The keynote here is self-control and good physical co-ordination, to regulate the writing movement. Such people are methodical, reliable and resistant to stress. Their emotional response is contained in moments of excitement or in awkward situations, where an unflappable attitude is of more use. They keep calm and composed, without actually becoming cold and indifferent – unless the script is also very leftward, in which case they are also inhibited, with a boring, constricted personality. In this case the script will also be narrow. The very regular writer tends to be restricted by tradition and needs time to adapt to changes which would affect his or her lifestyle.

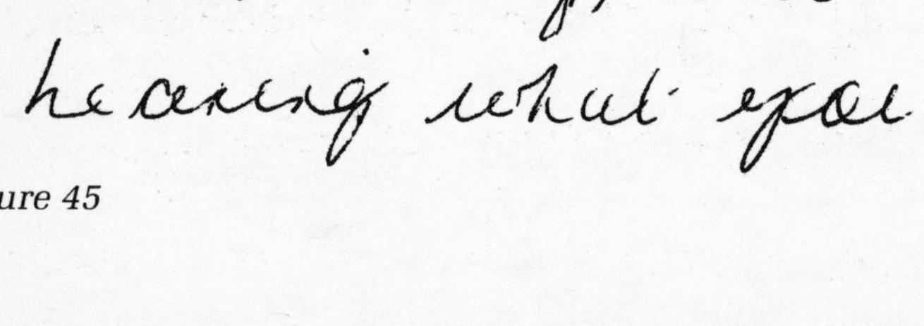

Figure 45

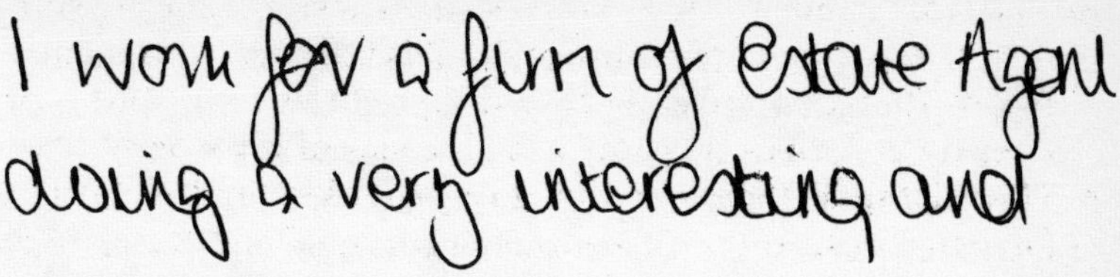

I work for a firm of Estate Agent
doing a very interesting and

Figure 46

Figures 45 and *46* are normal, regular scripts. Note the difference in width of the letter 'n'. This is a case of natural variation. The majority of the letters are narrow.

Too Regular
Writing which is too regular, like soldiers marching, is indicative of a very disciplined mind, unimaginative, often compulsive, slow and inflexible. Such writers can, however, have a strong sense of duty. Do not attach too much importance to this factor if the person is younger than the middle teens. As they mature, people develop a faster and less rigid style of script. *Figure 47* shows the writing of a teenager and *figure 48* that of an adult.

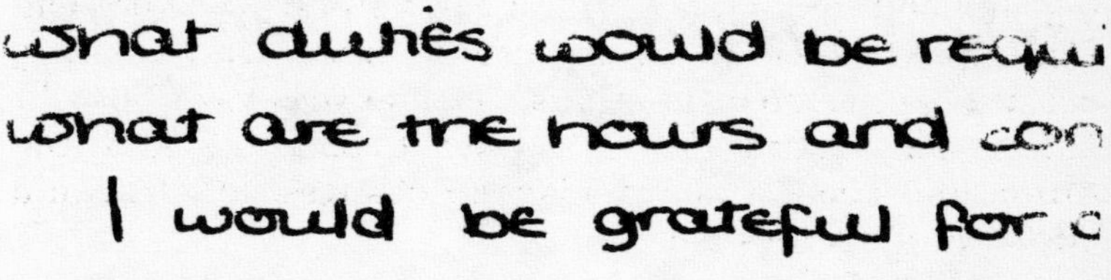

what duties would be requi
what are the hours and con
I would be grateful for a

Figure 47

e of my normal handwori
to hearing what you

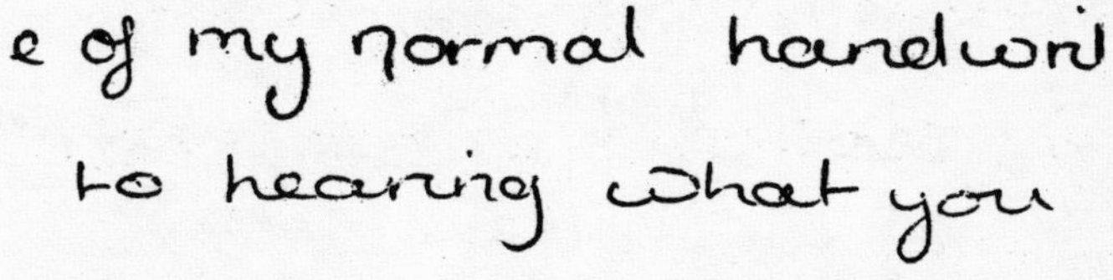

Figure 48

Irregular

Irregular writing is the natural expression of excitability, depending upon the Form Level. Where the Form Level is above average, there will be moderate emotional control, varied interests and the ability to adapt. A poor Form Level will point to a lack of control, an inconsistent behaviour pattern and a lack of positive direction and purpose – a writer who becomes caught up in his or her own feelings and is self-centred.

It is often only the middle zone that is slightly irregular, with an irregular distance in the down strokes and a slightly varying slant. In this case we have a sensitive person who neither clings to rigid principles nor suppresses excitement, and who will follow his or her instincts and aims without weakening. But a very irregular script (see *figures 49* and *50*) is negative; there is a lack of steadfastness in facing life and emotional weakness in the form of a lack of control over excitability; irritability, indecision and capricious mood levels are also indicated.

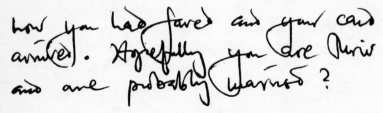

Figure 49

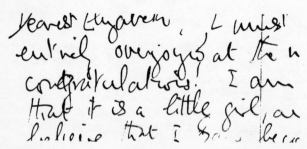

Figure 50

Such people tend to be swayed by the mood of the moment, rather than steadily pursuing their aims.

Normal irregularity (see *figures 51* and *52*) is not always apparent until the writing is closely examined. These writers are normally in control of their emotional response and have a balanced but flexible approach to life. Their minds need a varied, stimulating openness and mobility to cater for their creativity and sensitivity, with a spontaneity of mental assimilation. Often they are impulsive and impatient about progress, and will become irritable if allowed to stagnate. They are seldom contented.

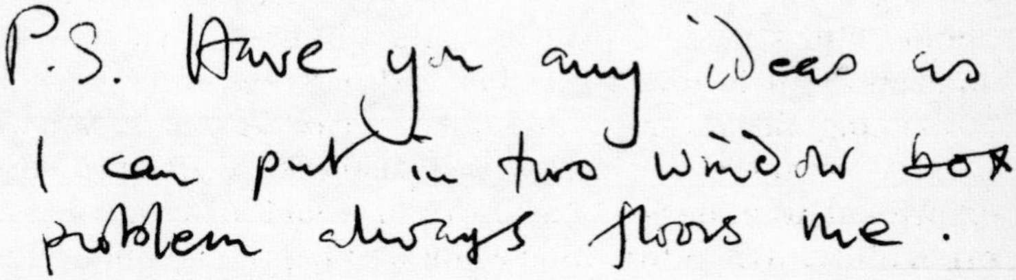

P.S. Have you any ideas as I can put in two window box problem always floors me.

Figure 51

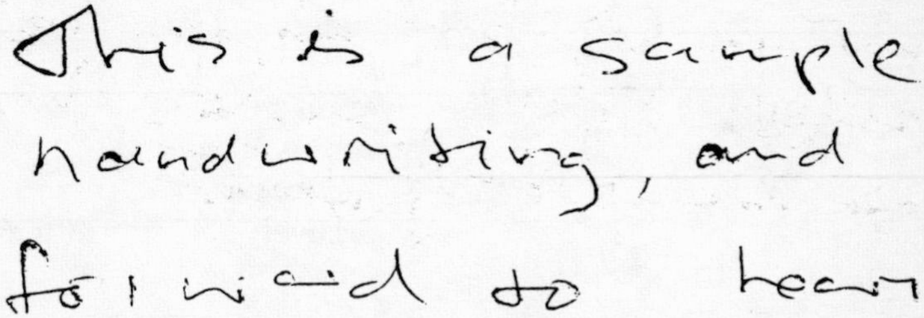

This is a sample handwriting, and forward to learn

Figure 52

Basically, regularity indicates a dominance of control and irregularity a dominance of emotion. There may be occasions when you are not sure because the writing is only slightly irregular: such individuals are moderately flexible mentally and have a positive control, but can be more emotionally responsive than regular writers (see *figures 53* and *54*).

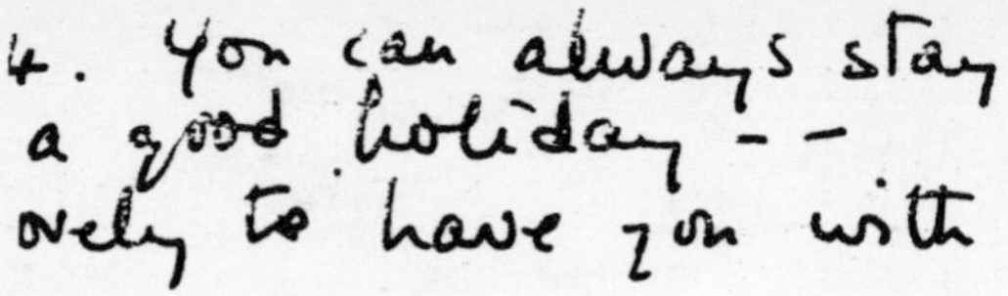

4. You can always stay
a good holiday --
only to have you with

Figure 53

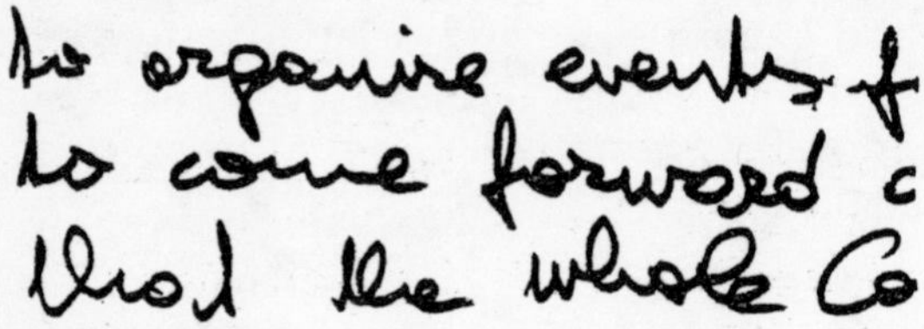

to organise events f
to come forword c
Urol the whole Co

Figure 54

The following are the main indications of regular and irregular writing.

Regular

Positive	*Negative (Rigid)*
Decisive	Monotonous
Stable	Dull
Orderly	Over-disciplined
Emotionally controlled	Emotionally cold
Calm	Stereotypical
Moderate	Excessively self-controlled
Possessing a strong sense of duty	Pedantic
	Inflexible
Reliable	Compulsive in habits
Enduring	Lacking spontaneity
Good at concentration	
Self-disciplined	

Irregular

Positive	Negative
Original in thought	Possessing undirected excitement
Possessing a lively mind	
Creative	Impulsive
Sensitive	Weak-willed
Open-minded	Easily distracted
Mobile	Confused in thought
Spontaneous	Fickle
Flexible and adaptable	Lacking balance
Having many interests	Unsettled
Good at problem-solving	Unpredictable
Strongly imaginative	Nervous and irritable
Restless, inspiring activity	Uneven in working capacity
	Easily influenced

RHYTHM

All writers have their own personal rhythm qualities, which are linked to the nervous functions of the whole system – the life force, tension and release, the ebb and flow of their vital energy.

Rhythm is not easy to evaluate because it cannot be measured. Dr Ludwig Klages called it 'that indefinable something' that can be understood only by intuition. It is best to hold the specimen of writing at a distance, turning it sideways and even upside down to get the overall flow without being influenced by the subject of the document. A good rhythm is neither too rigid nor too loose. The pen pressure and the control are balanced.

Think of children dancing. Some will have a natural ease of movement, the muscles tensing and relaxing with well-directed energy. Others will move awkwardly, possibly because of self-consciousness or inability to follow the guiding rhythm of the music. The result is that, although their movement is busy, it is jerky and wasteful of effort.

A *lively rhythm* (see *figures 55* and *56*) indicates good self-control, harmony in relationships, an economical use of

energy and effort and an acceptance of average tension-pro-
voking situations, with the ability to keep calm. There will
also be a harmonious co-ordination between the thought
process, which will be clear, and the controlled emotions,
resulting in a well-balanced personality without complexes,
ready to take a full part in life and face personal experiences
with perseverance in the face of difficulties.

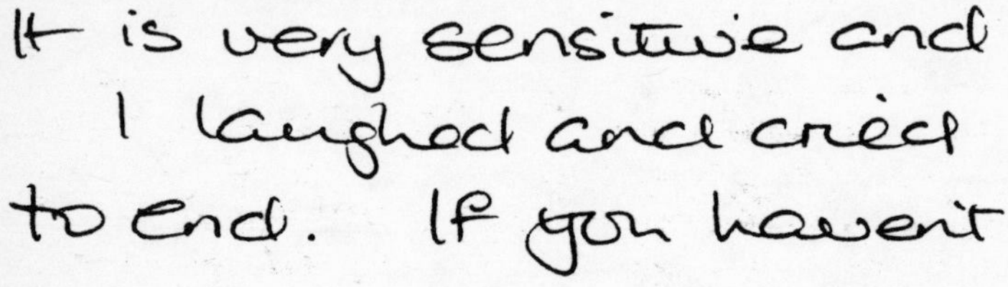

> It is very sensitive and
> I laughed and cried
> to end. If you haven't

Figure 55

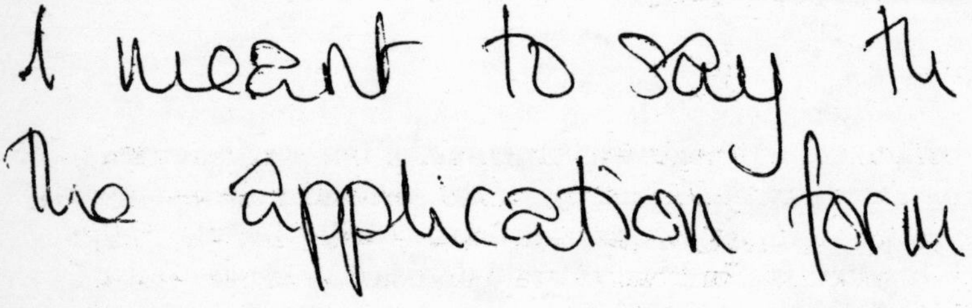

> I meant to say th
> The application form

Figure 56

A *poor rhythm* (see *figures 57* and *58*) shows an inharmo-
nious disturbance and rigidity, and combined with poor
Form Level indicates that the writer could be prone to emotional outbursts, with a lowered resistance to stress and tension. There may be an abrupt change in temperament and
these people get upset very easily. They are usually restless,
and always need variety and change, but can seldom achieve
satisfaction. They have very few friends because of their
inconsistent behaviour. They usually have the feeling that
they do not fit in, but are unable to do anything about it. Low
achievement becomes a fact of life for them.

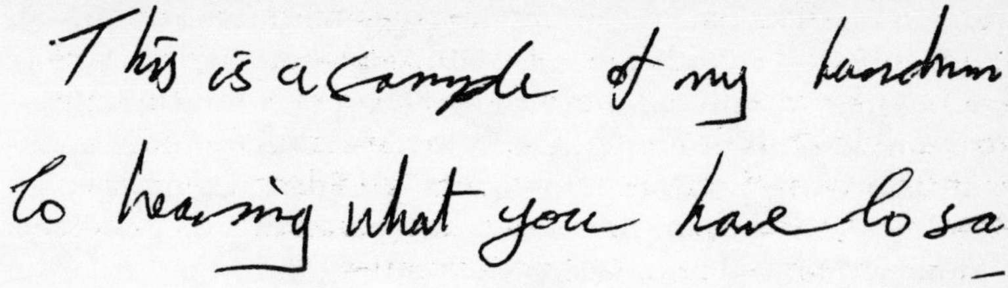

This is a sample of my handwriting

to hearing what you have to sa

Figure 57

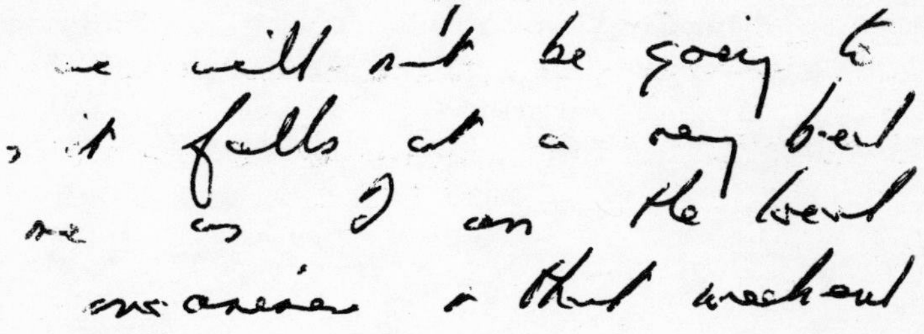

e will not be going to
, it falls at a very bad
as as I can the week
as answer a that weekend

Figure 58

Arrhythmic writing, which is irregular but shows a harmonious rhythmic quality with a good Form Level (see *figure 59*), indicates a restless person, but one who has the initiative to seek and find their ideals and hopes in life and use their imagination in artistic pursuits – a positive application of sensitivity, not particularly bound by tradition. Such writers are individualistic, but can cultivate friendship through a balanced expression of personality, in spite of their strong feelings. This is particularly true of the garland writer, whose disposition is to be friendly with everyone.

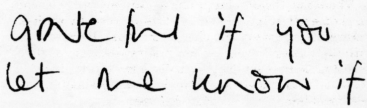

gate but if you
let me know if

Figure 59

Rhythm is associated with the degree of harmonious control over the letterforms, the expansion both vertically and horizontally, and slant variation. The productive organization of psychic energy (rhythm) and the degree of control or restlessness (regularity) are associated. Therefore the regularity indications need the assessment of rhythm to give them proper total value; the two go together and should be put into your own workbook: regularity first, then rhythm.

You must also remember that we are concerned with deviations from the copybook in all the writing trends, and rhythm and regularity are the most personal of these deviations. They give life to a script.

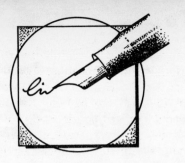

6 · SPEED AND FORM LEVEL

We've looked at the basics of Form Level already, but now we need to extend and deepen our understanding of this cardinal element of graphology. We'll start by looking at handwriting speed which is a key indicator of Form Level.

SPEED

A writer's personal tempo will normally be evident in his or her writing speed. It produces a natural graphic movement which reflects one's personality. Speed also has a bearing upon the writer's sincerity, mental spontaneity and action in relation to progress in life. One can tell whether a person is direct and open, with all dealings above board, or deviously unreliable. (Many habitual criminals write slowly and most have a poor Form Level.) Note that when referring to writing speed, I am not concerned with the speed of the signature, which can be very different from the writer's normal speed.

A high Form Level script, of which an essential part is speed, requires manual dexterity and experience which produces natural-looking, spontaneous writing. Leftwardness, unnecessary movements, ornamentation and any other inhibiting factors will be eliminated in a fast, smooth, natural writing (approximately 100 letters per minute). Even if the writing is fairly slow, there should be no deliberate deviation in the letterforms.

When the writer is trying to create an impression, usually in compensation for feelings of inferiority, the spontaneity will be inhibited and the writing will therefore look forced. This is not to say that genuine calligraphers – practitioners of the art of beautiful writing – are being devious or ostentatious. Such writers usually follow their artistic leanings and calligraphic training in their writing style. I am referring mainly to people who want to create an artistic impression but who, without the necessary experience and practice, make the writing look crude, false and over-flourished (see p. 42).

A person who is disabled through arthritis or other illness may not be able to write quickly even if their natural mental tendency would impel them to do so. In this case the letters will be slowly written and the forms simple and original. There may also be ataxic or shaky strokes. The tremulous quality will point to a manual disability, old age, or both.

Someone who is dyslexic may have letters and numbers pointing the wrong way, with a general messiness where hesitations appear as gaps or amendments. It should be obvious that this is not contrived writing, because the writing speed will be normal throughout, except for a few dyslexic indications.

If a slow writer has been forced to write more quickly than his natural pace, there will be noticeable weaknesses in certain areas, such as illegibility; also unstable connection such as threads. No one can write faster than their natural pace and still produce a spontaneous and legible piece of writing. Anonymous letter writers who endeavour to make it appear the letter is from a higher Form Level writer usually fail because they cannot copy the writer's speed.

Check the manuscript carefully for a change of tempo towards the end, indicating neglect; for example an impulsive, nervous, temperamental writer who is an unreliable finisher and cannot cope under stress. In a long manuscript the third or fourth page will be a more reliable guide to the writer's consistent staying power than the earlier pages.

Don't forget the envelope if it is available. This should be written legibly; if it is not, the writer has a lack of consideration for others, in this case the postman. Even when time is short, the envelope still needs to be written clearly; there is no point in using an indecipherable scribble when block letters can be written fairly fast.

To assess speed, various factors must be considered. For fast writing (see *figures 60* and *61*), examine the following:

- **Good connection**, with all letters connected
- **Garland** form with a wavy line or thread-type movement
- **Broad spacing** between words and letters
- **Pressure** consistently light to medium
- **Irregularity**
- **I-dots and t-bars** made to the right, omitted, or connected to the following letters
- **Left margin** widening down the page
- **Rightward slant** and other rightward tendencies
- **End strokes** extended rightward
- **Simplified writing**
- **Lines rising**, with a narrow right-hand margin
- A clean, clear **stroke** quality

A magnifying glass is recommended. Think of a clear, running stream, with a consistent flow.

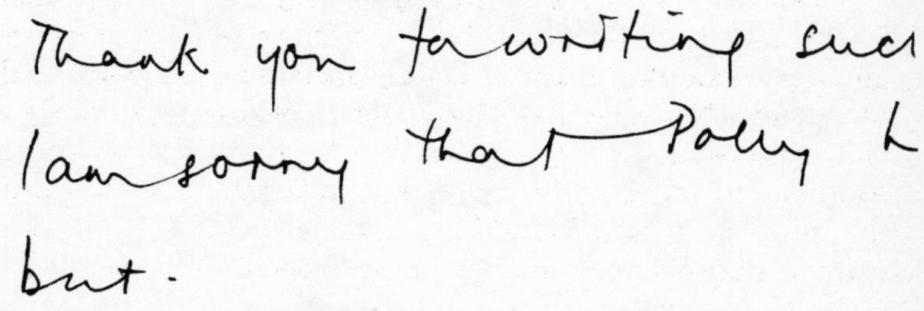

Figure 60

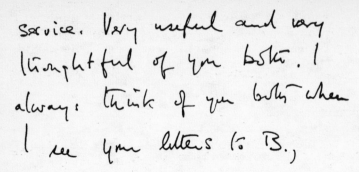

Figure 61

The following tendencies will indicate slow writing (see *figures 62* and *63*):

- Excessive **leftward** movements

- **Enrolments**

- Unnecessary **initial** and **terminal** strokes

- Extreme **narrowness**

- **Pen stops**

- Increasing **size** at the end of word

- Excessive **punctuation**

- Inconsistent **slant direction**

- **Amendments** to the letters

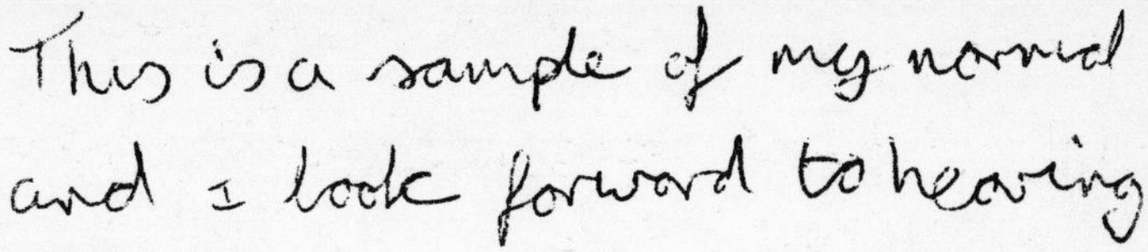

This is a sample of my normal and I look forward to hearing

Figure 62

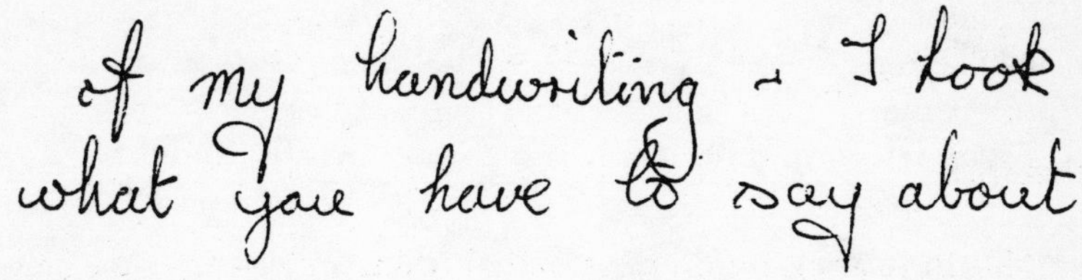

of my handwriting ~ I look what you have to say about

Figure 63

Writing of medium speed (see *figures 64* and *65*) strikes a happy medium between these extremes.

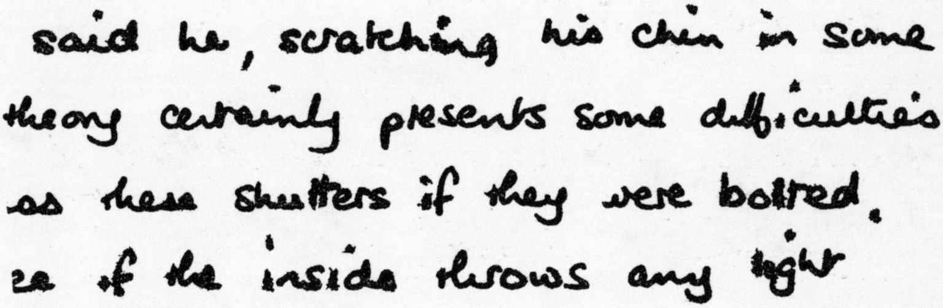

said he, scratching his chin in some theory certainly presents some difficulties as these shutters if they were bolted, ea of the inside throws any light

Figure 64

ng to our Telephone conversation I am very pleased to confirm Graphology by you, on

Figure 65

These are the main indications of the various writing speeds:

Fast speed

Positive	*Negative*
Quick but legible	Quick and illegible
Natural	Impatient and hasty
Mentally agile	Irritable over trifles
Extrovert	Easily distracted
Purposeful	Lacking consideration
Industrious	Inconsistent
Progressive in functioning	Superficial in thought

Medium speed

Positive
Sincere
Reliable
Careful in thought
Good at organizing

Slow speed

Positive	*Negative (poor Form Level)*
Steady and careful	Lazy
Self-controlled	Slow-thinking
Considerate	Dull
Introvert	Indecisive
Determined	Weak-willed
Thoughtful	Unreliable
Financially prudent	Lacking integrity

Do not neglect writing speed in your assessment. Practise as much as you can and you will come to realize its importance in an analysis. It is also essential for the correct assessment of Form Level.

FORM LEVEL

Form Level is a very important aspect of graphology because the meaning of every other writing trend depends upon it. Form Level – abbreviated to F/L – is defined as the indication of the writer's degree of intellectual capacity, creative potential, level of general intelligence, educational background and capacity, and the adherence to moral principles.

Its significance is as a pointer to whether the writing you are analysing is to be assessed as negative or positive. It is not dependent upon cultural background – good taste, for example, can be inborn – but is more the positive use of effort and ability in whatever area it occurs.

A person of high intelligence (high F/L), who is able to assess what is important in life, will react differently from a person of much lower intellect (low F/L), who is ruled by instinct rather than reason, and who might therefore react rashly and without forethought. In such a case, the signs in the writing might be ugly exaggerations, with no genuine originality, poor spacing, mixed slant and either great irregularity or rigidity, and the sample might give a dirty overall impression. However, you will seldom get a sample of handwriting quite this inferior!

Where a lack of integrity is suspected, always check for at least *five* indications (see pp. 101–2). Before arriving at this stage, you should have had a lot of practice on a variety of writings, on which you should have kept the analysis simple, to avoid errors.

It is critical that you are totally familiar with the working out of Form Level, this essential writing element which is a crucial part of the whole assessment. You can only do this by constant practice until it is second nature whenever you see a handwriting sample. F/L embodies all you have learned so far, which is why I have left it until now.

There are three factors involved in F/L: speed, spacing and originality. We have already covered the first factor: speed rating, which indicates spontaneity for intellectual capacity and sincerity. The second factor, spacing, should now be assessed for intelligence.

- **Margins and general arrangement of the text on the page** It should be neither crowded nor excessively open.
- **Intervals between the words** Are they clear and of equal length?
- **Distance between the lines of writing** Is it too wide or too narrow? Is there any mingling or is the distance even? Are the lines straight?

Originality
Finally, the third factor is the originality of the letterforms.

- Are they copybook, or do they deviate?
- Are they graceful, or vulgar, simplified or not?
- Are they legible?

Assess each factor as high, medium or low on your worksheet. The average F/L writer will be a good all-rounder, who has an intelligent response to life, but is not brilliant intellectually.

Examples of high F/L are shown in *figures 66–70*.

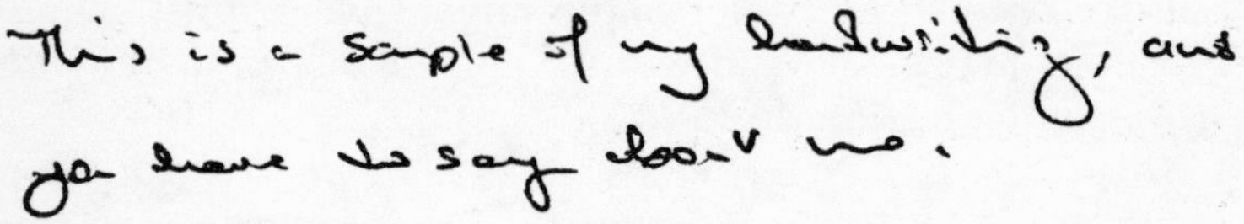

Figure 66

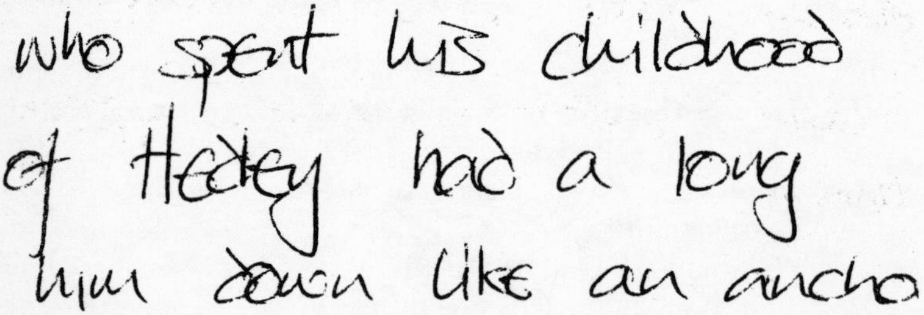

Figure 67

you very much for the presents you gave us all as. I can't tell you James enjoys playing his

Figure 68

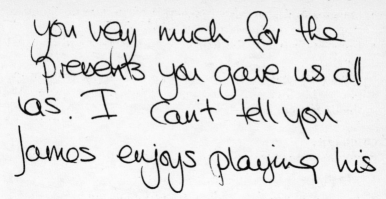

Figure 69

Thanks again for an excellent last week — .... much appreci

Figure 70

Figures 71–5 are examples of medium F/L.

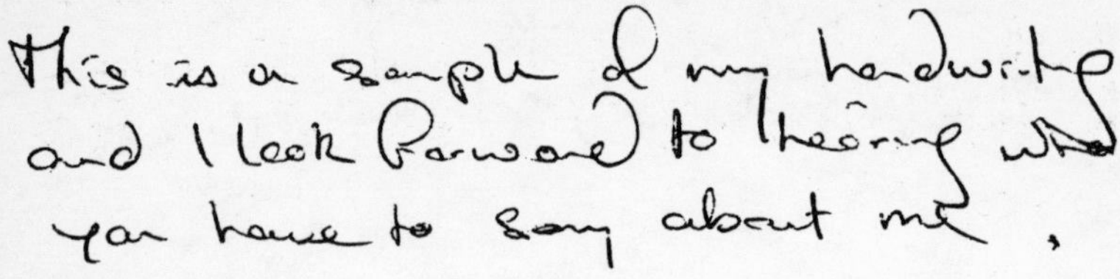

This is a sample of my handwriting
and I look forward to hearing what
you have to say about me ,

Figure 71

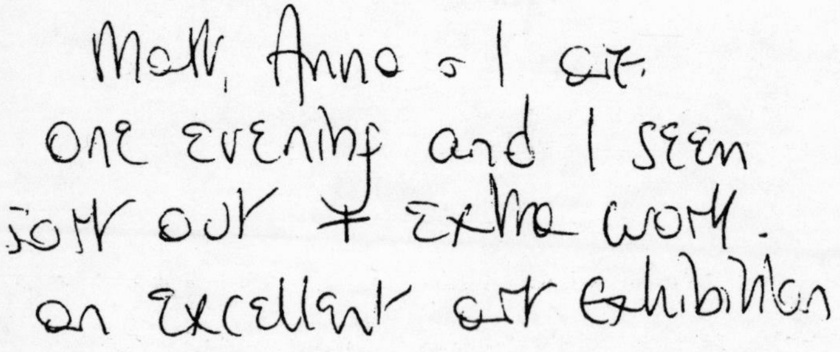

Matt, Anna & I sit.
one evening and I seen
joan out & extra work.
an excellent art exhibition

Figure 72

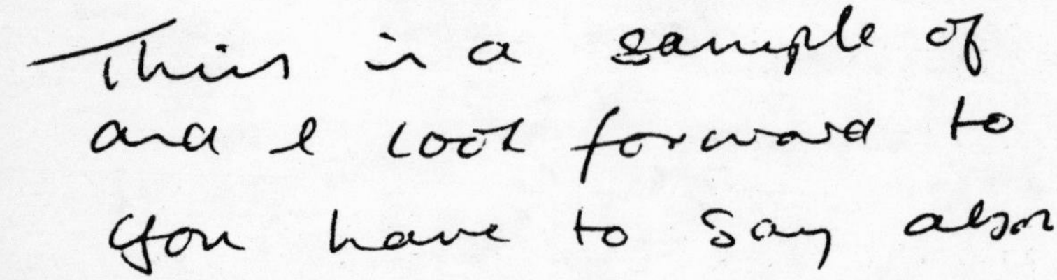

This in a sample of
and I look forward to
you have to say also

Figure 73

We had a lovely hol
Staying in a chalet —
of joyous secluded bea

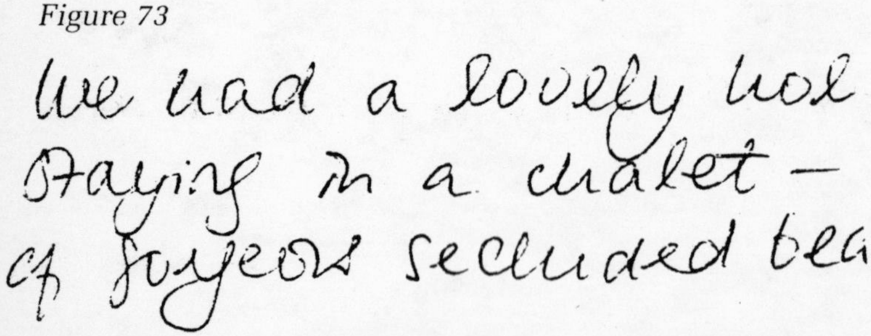

Figure 74

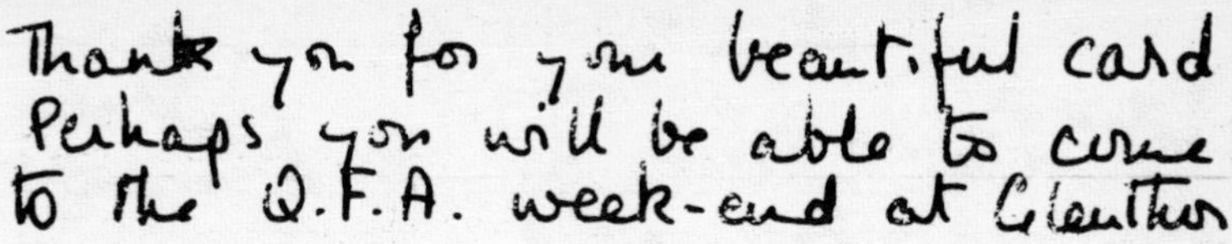

Thank you for your beautiful card
Perhaps you will be able to come
to the Q.F.A. week-end at Gleuthor

Figure 75

Examples of low F/L are shown in figures 76–80.

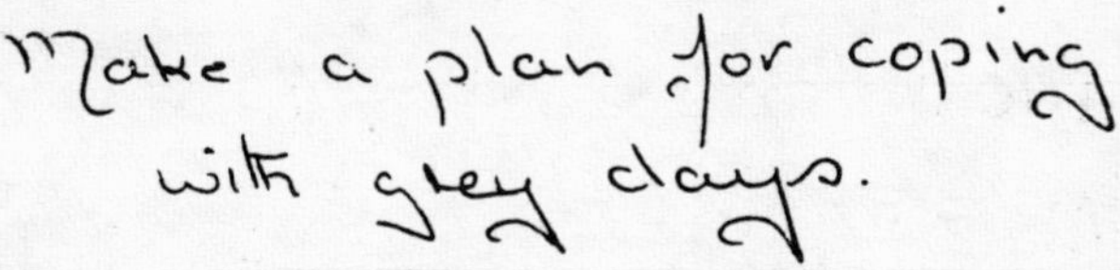

Make a plan for coping
with grey days.

Figure 76

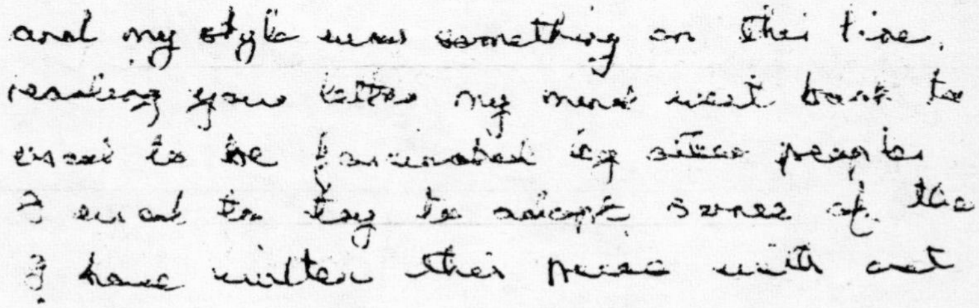

and my style was something on this line.
reading your letter my mind went back to
used to be fascinated by such people
I used to try to adopt some of the
I have written their piece with out

Figure 77

handwriting and I Look

you have to say about me

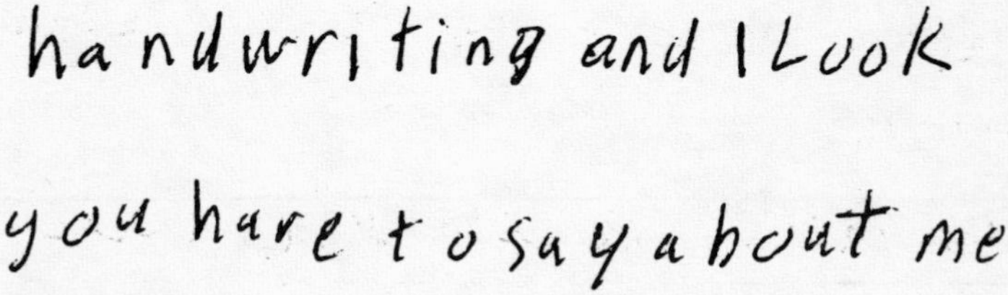

Figure 78

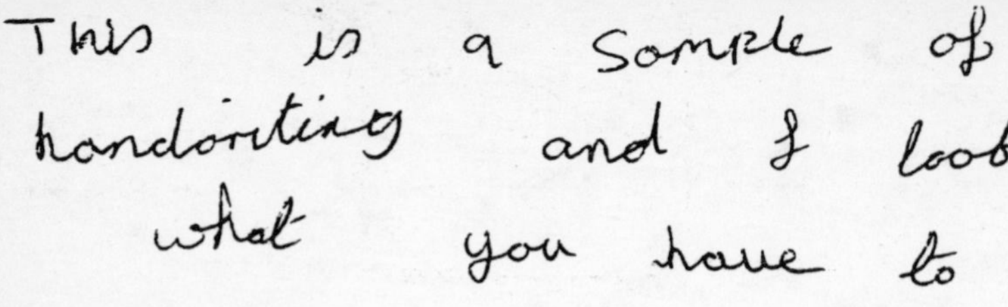

This is a sample of
handwriting and I look
what you have to

Figure 79

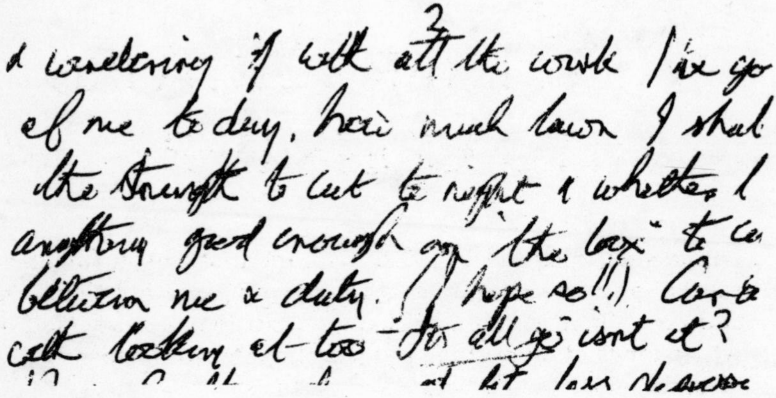

Figure 80

Only your own experience and practice will tell you where to draw the line between high, medium and low Form Levels.

7 · OTHER FACTORS TO CONSIDER

Capitals, especially the capital 'I' for the first person singular, can be very revealing, as can the ways people dot their 'i's and cross their 't's. In this chapter we'll look at these and a whole range of other small but significant features that you'll need to note in a comprehensive analysis.

CAPITALS

Here we are discussing capital letters in relation to the size of the writing.

To some people, the word 'capital' suggests importance and the way people write capitals reflects the way they see themselves. Self-important people are often compensating for their own feelings of inferiority, and this is evident in their writing in the form of very large, unusually wide capitals – higher than the tops of letters with normal upstrokes (ascenders) such as in 'd', 'b', 'l' etc.

In addition, ornate capitals will indicate status-seeking. Where the capital letters are crudely overdone, the writer will probably be as ostentatious in real life, in an attempt to further his or her self-esteem, an aim which is rarely achieved.

Small, simple capitals, with no ornamentation, are the opposite of the above, and show an unassuming, genuine personality, sympathetic and probably with a satisfactory lifestyle. Having no need for false projection, such writers prefer to remain in the background and are valuable, unobtrusive workers.

Plain, large capitals in a proportionate middle zone (large writing) indicate an ambitious person who may be creative, with a need to pursue a direct approach, but who desires recognition for his or her efforts, like the show-business personality type.

Small printed capitals indicate a literary mind with no pretence or time for ambitious projection. Such writers' interests are usually intellectual.

Capital letters are sometimes written inside a word. Such writers will make more of a situation than it warrants. However, if the only capital inside a word is the letter 'k' then it should be disregarded, because many people do this.

Too many capital letters used inappropriately indicate a compulsive writer with no concept of what is, and what is not, important.

Tall, narrow capitals point to an introverted writer who is sensitive and may have spiritual interests. Reserve, particularly where the slant is leftward, restricts ambition. There may be occasions when this type of capital letter is made taller by an extra stroke – amended. This indicates a desire for an improvement in the writer's lifestyle, which is rarely achieved. These people are prone to feelings of anxiety.

Generally, wide capitals indicate an outgoing, self-reliant writer. Illustrated here are just a few varied styles of the capital letter 'T' only.

THE PERSONAL PRONOUN 'I'

The personal pronoun 'I' (PPI) has a greater significance than other capitals. Other capital letters reflect how we see ourselves in a social situation and our intention to be noticed, or not, whereas the PPI is related to our secret selves. It manifests itself through the Ego (C G Jung), the inner centre of our personality.

This single letter must be assessed accurately for any variance from the rest of the script, particularly pressure, size, form, slant and placement in relation to other words. A separate section should be provided for it in your own graphology workbook – add to it as you read more books, but always consider what is being said against your own experience – if not immediately, then later.

Figures 81–92 show a variety of styles of the PPI, which can be interpreted as follows:

89

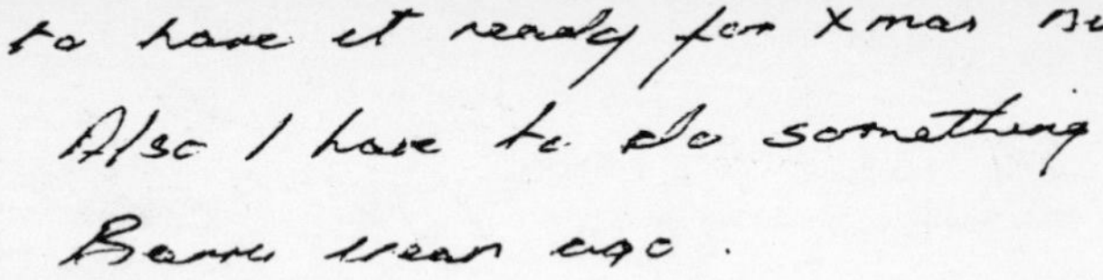

to have it ready for Xmas but Also I have to do something Some years ago.

Figure 81: the **same size** as the script in general. Moderately self-confident, practical and objective.

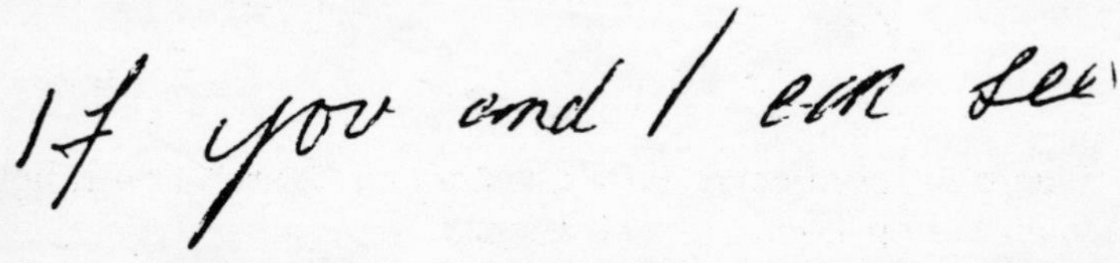

If you and I can see

Figure 82: **taller** than the general script, including capitals. A secret desire to dominate – usually compensating for feelings of inferiority.

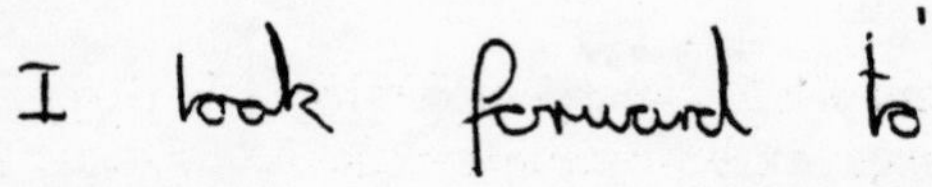

I look forward to

Figure 83: **smaller** than the script. No desire for personal superiority over others; possibly lack of self-confidence.

and I look

Figure 84: **open and wide.** Strong imagination; feeling of self-worth and desire to further contacts with others.

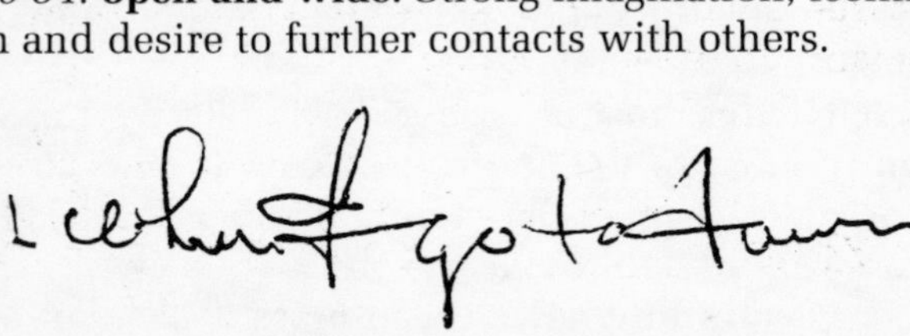

I what go to town

Figure 85: **flourished**. Poor taste, lack of refinement; vulgar expressive impulses; deep-rooted inferiority feelings which are not allowed to surface in company.

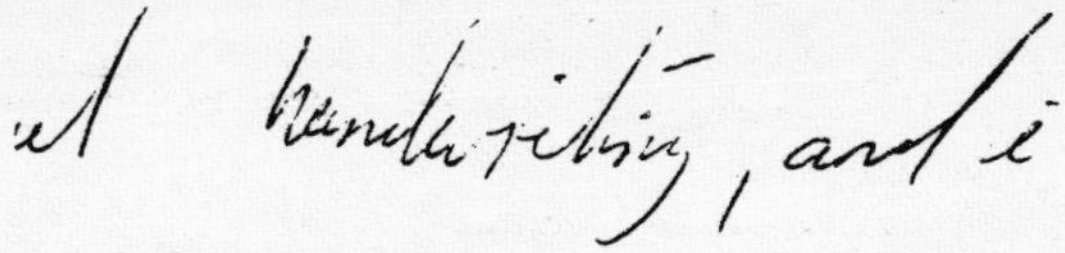

Figure 86: **like a small dotted 'i'**: Serious lack of self-esteem; immature attitude; humility.

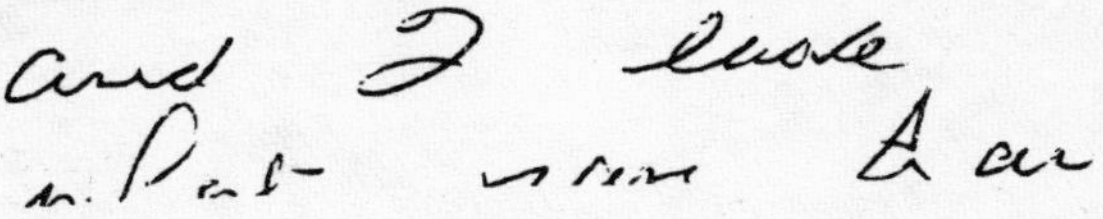

Figure 87: similar to the old-fashioned **figure 2**, with bottom loop. Very prudent, security conscious.

Figure 88: **enrolled**. Greedy and miserable disposition if very small; if large, independent; hides emotions; reluctant to relate intimately.

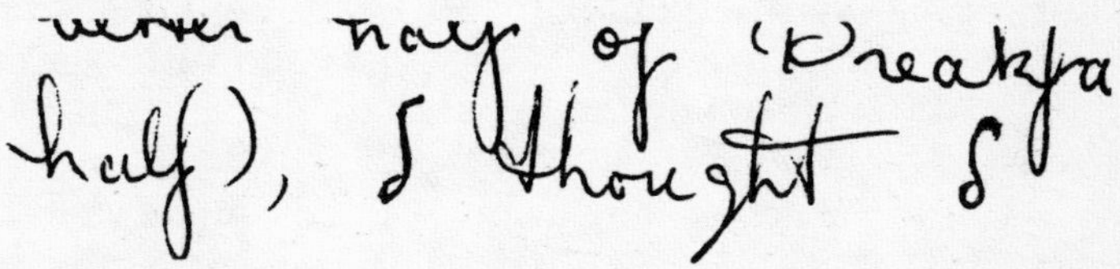

Figure 89: **heavy pressure** in a PPI in otherwise normal or weak-pressured writing. Tension, a constant fear of the future and reluctance to progress further.

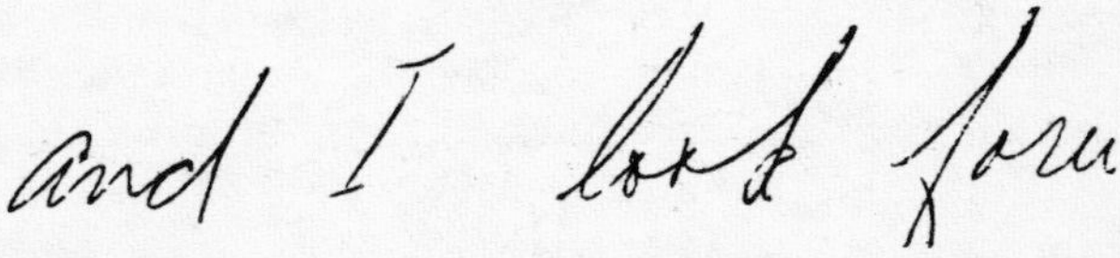

Figure 90: a **wider than normal gap** between the PPI and the next word. Fear of isolation, but also fear of mixing socially.

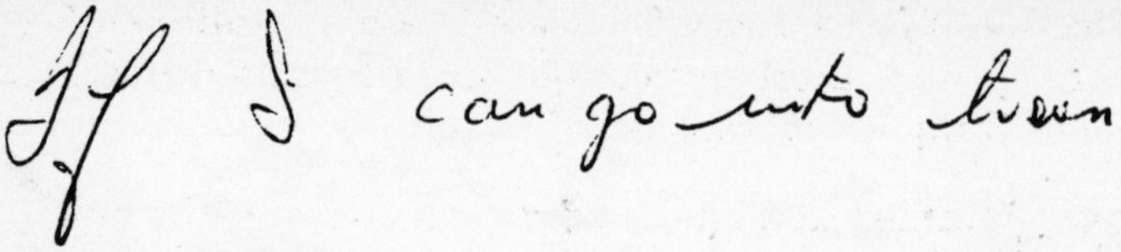

Figure 91: PPI **slanted leftward in an upright or rightward-slanted script**. Feelings of inhibition kept secret and/or guilty feelings in a sexual or religious context.

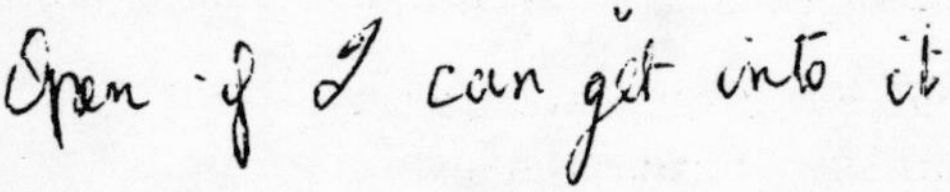

Figure 92: **rightward slant in a leftward-slanted or upright script**. Conflict of emotions caused by a tendency to suppress secret feelings of an outgoing impulse and a fear of social involvement.

I-DOTS AND T-BARS

If i-dots and t-bars are assessed without considering other factors, mistaken personality and character traits could result. It is therefore best to use the i-dots and t-bars for confirmation of traits already found rather than coming to a conclusion based on them alone.

Ask yourself whether they fit in with the general rhythmic movement, or whether the t-bars in particular are very conspicuous with heavy pressure, or with leftward movements and with the bar itself longer than normal.

A very dominant t-bar on or above the stem, sloping upwards, indicates ambition, determination and the willpower to succeed in the face of adverse conditions. A weak t-bar suggests sensitivity. The length will determine the amount of ambition, but the drive will not be so intense; nor will the writer be so aggressive in attitude.

Note the position of the i-dot – whether it is high or low over the letter stem. If all the i-dots are exactly in line, it suggests a careful, but possibly boring, writer, particularly if the t-bars are light, short and balanced half way up the stem.

The variety of i-dots and t-bars is almost infinite. A few examples with their indications are illustrated here. Add them to your own workbook.

Circle i-dot, often found in the writing of young girls with a desire to create an impression of sophistication. In adults (except in Swedish writing), false intellectual projection and ostentatious behaviour to create an effect; in stylish, high F/L writing, design and artistic endeavour

High and rightward-directed i-dot Socially outgoing inclinations.

i-dot omitted In a poor F/L script, forgetfulness and perhaps carelessness; in medium to high F/L, omitted for expediency.

i-dot to the left Cautiousness.

Tick-like i-dot open to the right An observant person with quick-acting initiative.

i-dot forming a connection with the next letter Mental agility; tendency not to waste time or effort.

t-bar connected to the next letter As above.

t-bar with heavy pressure, pointing downwards Fixed opinions; sulky and unco-operative.

t-bar with heavy thick ending Aggressive and could be violent.

t-bar near the base of the stem Lack of self-confidence and feelings of inferiority in company – particularly when leftward on the stem, probably in copybook-style script.

t-bar rightward and disconnected Motivated by ambition; strong initiative, but could cut corners for expediency; irritable when inactive.

t-bar leftward and disconnected Indecisive; mind occupied with past issues; slow.

Hooked t-bar in a rightward slant Determination in getting own way; if the slant is leftward could also indicate awkwardness.

Star-shaped t-bar Usually thorough, but can be obstinate and cantankerous; opposition to any personal interference.

Knotted t-bar Someone who likes to be accurate over small details; old-fashioned attitude; good time-keeper; reliable.

Do not assess a single i-dot or t-bar as dominant if the majority are different – for example, 1 very long t-bar among 14 short ones is an isolated factor; the short t-bar will be dominant in this case.

PUNCTUATION

A careful person who is considerate to the reader will place full stops and commas only where they are required and will also break the continuity of the writing with paragraphs. People who use excessive punctuation are in need of educational guidance or else are trying to create an impression of importance.

Underlying heavy pressure points to a neurotic personality who needs to have the last word and overrides any criticisms. Such people will often finish a sentence for you while you are talking. Whatever anyone else has achieved, they have done better. Their commas will be longer than normal and their exclamation and question marks large. They lack common sense.

Where punctuation is omitted in fast writing, it is for the sake of expediency – it is the sign of a busy person who has no time for irrelevant issues. The Form Level will probably be high.

Missing commas and full stops in slow writing indicates a

neglectful person with a poor education. The Form Level will be low.

Make a point of indicating the punctuation intelligence level on your worksheet. In this way you will learn always to include it in your examination of a script.

THE SIGNATURE

Like the PPI (see p. 89) the signature is also an Ego projection but this time it reveals how the writer wishes to be seen: it is, in effect, a show card. It is important to understand this because the signature and the writing can often be at variance. The signature alone should therefore not on any account be analysed without a sample of the writing.

If, through changing circumstances, the lifestyle or the writer's self-image alters, then the signature will almost certainly very slowly alter to reflect the new image. This change can only be detected when old signatures are available for comparison, showing the degree and the form of alteration. This is of great importance when, for instance, a forged will is suspected and the signature on it does not correspond to the style of another signature dating from an earlier period. However, I should emphasize that such things as suspect document examination are very specialized and beyond the scope of this book.

A show-business personality, on reaching 'star' status, may contrive a stylish signature for autographs, but still retain his or her previous one for important personal documents and cheques. But if the signature is different from the writing in the case of a person who is not in the public eye and who should have no need to appear different, it indicates that he or she is putting on a façade – a false representation – the degree of which will be shown in the amount of variation between handwriting and signature. The more important a writer is trying to appear, the larger the signature.

When a person has to write a form of signature many times a day, like a bank cashier or doctor, it will be purely a mark of recognition and not a proper signature with which he or she would sign documents of importance.

When the handwriting is leftward-slanted and the signature rightward-slanted (see *figure 93*) the writer is trying to appear as an extrovert, although inwardly he or she is of an introverted nature.

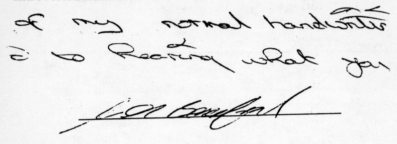

Figure 93

When the opposite is found, it indicates the reverse (see *figure 94*).

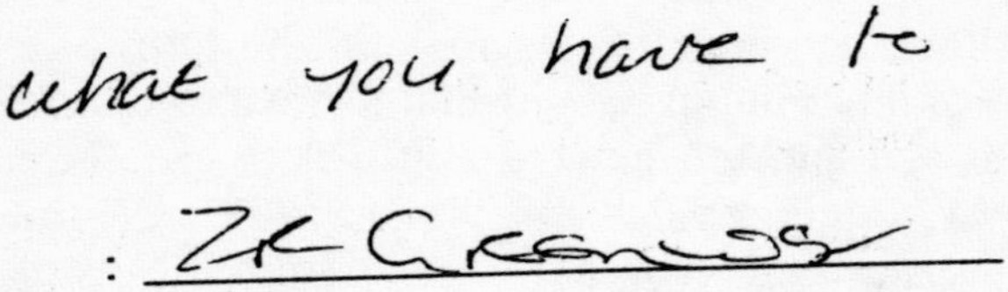

Figure 94

A signature which is smaller than the script indicates a mild-mannered person who wishes to remain unobserved. When the handwriting and smaller signature are both slanted leftwards (see *figure 95*), it indicates a very introverted personality, particularly when the handwriting is narrow.

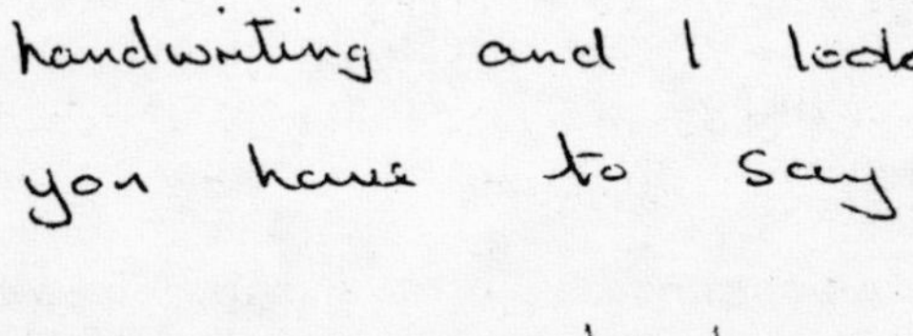

Figure 95

A signature which is noticeably larger than the script and rightward-slanting (see *figure 96*) indicates an extrovert personality, particularly when the writing is wide. The larger the actual script in relation to the larger signature and the more flamboyant, the more outgoing the person is and the more attention is desired.

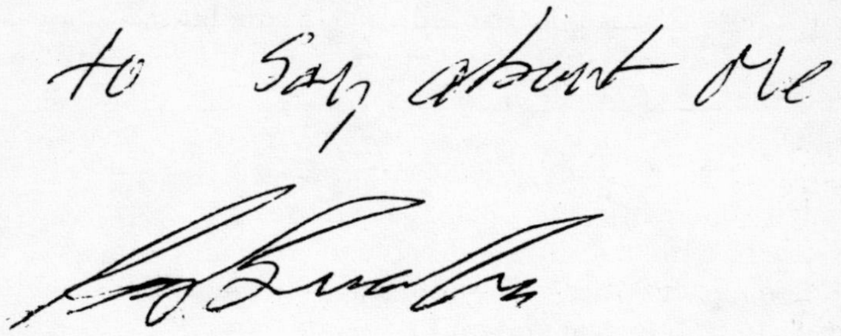

Figure 96

An illegible signature, the mark of a business person, can indicate secretiveness when there are enrolments and evasiveness if it is also very thread-like. Both are evident in *figure 97*. When there are also threads in the script itself, the writer has a shrewd understanding of people and is often able to manipulate them subtly into acceding willingly to his requests.

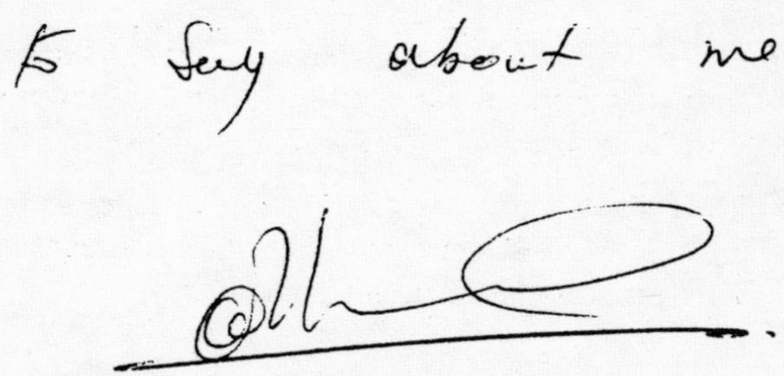

Figure 97

An enrolled signature (see *figure 98*) points to a writer who wishes to remain isolated from social contact. It may indicate total resignation, particularly if it is leftward-slanted with widely-spaced words (denoting withdrawal) and if the entire signature is crossed out.

Figure 98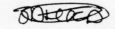

An underlined signature indicates an ambitious person – more so if the line is straight and rising. If the underlining is scroll-shaped or ornate in any way, it is a sign of affectation (a show-off). An underlining consisting of several sharp, long strokes indicates an aggressive and assertive attitude. A straight underlining of normal pressure, not too long, suggests self-confidence without being overbearing.

When the first name is prominent and legible, the writer wishes to be informal and on first name terms.

Examine the signature in the same way as you did the PPI. In addition, note the direction of the terminal stroke in relation to the rightward and leftward factors. Remember, in old age the signature can be more fluent than the writing in a letter, because the signature is practised more.

LOWER EXTENSIONS AND LOOPS

As we have seen, the lower zone is the area of instinct, so sexual response is related to this zone, and the form of letters in it is important to determine how sexual response is manifested.

The down stroke represents energy (pressure) and the actual loop imagination. This interpretation is applicable to the alphabets of most countries. Some examples are as follows:

 Nervous disorders and odd sexual habits

 Sadistic and masochistic inclination

Homosexual tendencies, male or female

 Sexual inhibition and fear

 Sexually imaginative

Short broken loop: sexual fear; conventional code of behaviour in this respect

A lack of sexual interest

Strictly conventional sexual practices; can be boring but orthodox

Seen mainly in very young girls – romantic ideas; will respond to affection rather than sex itself

Abnormal sexual interests relating to self-indulgence

 Sexually repressed and disappointed – can also tend towards high moral standards; sexual frustration can result in aggressive tendencies; usually found in mature female handwriting – if found in a male script, writer could be difficult to live with, due to pettiness

Usually found in a male writing – mother-orientated and afraid to approach a female, unless for social activities only; not sexually experienced or outgoing

 Caring attitude to love and sexual expression

 A sexual tease; self-gratification preferred

 Strong physical desires and sensual feelings

 Avoidance of sexual responsibility; often a hoarder and greedy

 Sex-drive stifled – usually a young person, not yet mature

 Can be critical and hypersensitive; sexual avoidance whenever an excuse can be found

 Sexual restlessness; vulnerable to suggestion from a person of a stronger personality

 Will not discuss sexual feelings; inhibited

Male with dominant attitude towards women or argumentative female, also prudish

 Sexual energy sublimation into social activity as a technique of avoidance

 Sexual disturbances due to deep anxiety problems

DISHONESTY

In matters relating to personnel selection you would usually be expected to give an opinion on the integrity of the applicant. But before you attempt to include traits characterizing dishonesty in an analysis, several years' experience in graphology is essential, considering how important your opinion can be for the people involved. And a full worksheet should be completed before you consider any signs of dishonesty.

There are, of course, many forms of dishonesty but here we are dealing only with criminality – stealing. And any indications you find will not necessarily mean the person concerned would actually steal. The inclination to do so is usually suppressed, by a fear of the trouble it could cause.

A poor Form Level, poor rhythmic quality and a slow speed (in a graphically mature writer, so not due to old age or illness) will be the first pointers you will notice. After that, look for the following indications. Owing to limitations of space, only a few factors can be listed here, and they are not presented in order of importance. At the very least there must be five indications and preferably more.

- **A weak, thready script** – open to influence
- **Ambiguous letterforms** – imbalance of outlook and needs
- **Touching-up** of letter strokes throughout – trying to give a false impression, but producing further illegibility

- **Blotched writing**, or writing punctuated by **pen rests** (shown by dots) – uncontrolled activity and strain
- Each letter written **with three or four separate strokes** instead of the usual one or two – lack of co-operation
- **Circular letters open at the base** – will act contrary to convention and is open to selfish behaviour
- **Extreme narrowness**, covering strokes in all three zones – concealment
- **A very low upper zone**, where a small letter 'd' looks like a copybook 'a' because there is very little stem – lack of spiritual or moral values
- **A constantly changing slant** – unresolved inner conflicts
- Many **leftward terminal strokes** which break the rhythm, especially in the middle and lower zones – lack of responsibility
- **Incomplete terminals**, that is, strokes which should, but do not, reach the baseline, not due to carelessness in a normal script – may appear friendly, but is not really so
- A **marked difference between the signature and the script**, the signature possibly being ornate – a variation between the writer's self-image and his or her actual behaviour

You are not likely to have any handwriting samples to hand in which you can see all these factors of unreliability together. You should, of course, add them to your own workbook.

Add unreliability factors to your assessment only when and where it is relevant to do so and use a reference number to maintain essential confidentiality rather than a name for the analysis, in case it accidentally falls into the wrong hands.

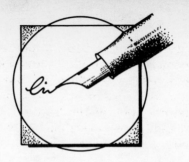

8 · THE WORKSHEET AND ANALYSIS

PUTTING YOUR KNOWLEDGE INTO PRACTICE

We're now going to work through a complete sample of handwriting. We'll practise setting up your worksheet and then look at how you might proceed to its analysis.

THE WORKSHEET

The worksheet that follows, which is based on the letter in *figure 99*, will demonstrate how you should collate your information. It is in the order in which you have worked through this book, step by step. This will help to ensure that you leave nothing out in your own worksheet, and that it also follows this order.

10,

Bath.

20·9-94

Dear Jean

Thank you for your letter received today. Time has gone very quickly since your last letter in April.

Pleased to hear all the news, and the places you visited during the summer.

I have been to Scotland many times the reflections

in the water at Loch Merve and all the colours of the
Jurriday Mountains when the sun shone on them. I shall
never forget.

I am going to Wales the lent week in September.

No hope the good weather holds out.

I will write again when I get home and give
you all the news.

Love from
Margaret.

Figure 99

Initial Information

The writer is female, aged approximately 48, British, and therefore taught the English copybook. The letter being analysed was written with a ballpoint pen on a good quality white paper.

1 Size

Absolute – all three zones. The average is 9mm – normal.

No special significance.

2 Zones

Upper (U/Z): the average measurement is 5mm dominant.

Middle (M/Z): the average measurement is 2mm – small.

Lower (L/Z): the average measurement is 3mm including the last stroke of the letter 'm', which goes into the L/Z – normal.

There is a moderate degree of interest in intellectual subjects.

The imagination is realistic.

Strong ideals.

Modest personality.

Not particularly interested in social activity.

Practical inclinations.

3 Slant

Upright with slight deviation leftwards.

A calm, cool attitude is maintained.

Self-sufficient and reliable; reserved personality expression.

The ability to reason.

4 Width

Normal, with some narrowness in the U/Z

Cautious over plans and ideas.

Good self-control.

Aware of economic necessity.

5 Degree of connection

Mainly connected.

Logical thinker; must work within a system.

Co-operative in a team, but also independent.

6 Form of connection

Mainly copybook U/Z and M/Z.

Normal thinking process.
Needs to be clearly
 understood in
 communication.
Predictable. Can be formal in
 approach.
Strong traditional values.
Slow to adapt to new ideas
 which must be proven.
Rather rigid attitude to
 sexual subjects.

7 Letterform

Mainly copybook.

No special significance
 not already covered.

8 Shading

Slight sharpness but no significant
dominant.

Good self-discipline.
Spiritual awareness.

9 Pressure

Light U/Z and M/Z, with some
medium heavy pressure in the
L/Z down strokes.

Sensitive. Could be slightly
 possessive in relationships.
Good self-control and a fairly
 strong willpower.

10 Initial and terminal strokes

Copybook initial and terminal
strokes with some heavy long
terminals penetrating the L/Z
(towards the self).

Requires a normal amount
 of time to prepare for
 action.
Can be very determined not
 to be influenced by others.
Can be stubborn.

11 Margins

Narrow left margin.
Slightly wide at the bottom of the
 right hand margin.
Slightly wide top margin.
Slightly cramped signature.

There is a tendency to be
 influenced by the past.
Wary with regard to
 progressive pursuits. Prone
 to be somewhat fearful of
 the future.

12 Distance between words and lines

Normal to slightly wide, and inconsistent spacing.

Good organization of time and effort.
Slightly withdrawn in relationships.
Constructive thinking processes. Good sense of justice.

13 Line direction

There is a slight inconsistency in the line direction. However, they are clearly separate; there is therefore no dominant.

The writer was suffering from slight fatigue at time of writing.

14 Regularity

Very slightly irregular.

In control of emotional responses, with a balanced approach to life.
There is sensitivity, which could lead to slight irritability and restlessness when under pressure.

15 Rhythm

There is a fairly lively rhythm with a slightly stilted quality.

See the regularity assessment above.

16 Speed

	Fast	Slow	
Connection	✓		The key words here are average and positive.
Garland		✓	
Spacing	✓		Sincere, reliable.
Pressure	✓		Careful thinker.
Regularity		✓	Good organizer.
i-dots, t-bars		✓	Steady and careful.
Left margin	✓	✓	Considerate.
Rightward slant	✓	✓	Thoughtful.
End stroke		✓	Financially prudent.
Simplicity		✓	No devious intention or inclination.
Direction of lines		✓	
Firmness of stroke	✓		Everything must be 'above board'.
	6	8	

Needs time to assimilate
information.
Will remember adequately.

NOTE: Where there are two ticks, for one factor, it means that neither characteristic is predominant. When that happens you can also leave the boxes blank. In both cases one will cancel out the other.

AVERAGE SPEED: neither fast nor too slow.

---

17 Form level

- **Speed**: Average
- **Spacing**:
  General arrangement
  and margins good
  Spacing between words slightly
  inconsistent but good
  Spacing between lines slightly
  inconsistent but clear – good
- **Assessment of spacing**: Average
- **Originality**
  Copybook forms low to average
  Simplicity high
  Legibility good

An average intellect, not brilliant but practical and well balanced.
There are no complexes or deviant patterns of behaviour. A reliable worker who will use common sense in determining what is and what is not important.
Natural and genuine respect for others.
No time for daydreams.
Average artistic awareness and practical application.

This warrants a positive evaluation of the factors in the handwriting, since there are no negative indications; but bear in mind the general educational standard is average.

Overall form level: average.

---

18 Capitals

Normal in this script and normal in relation to the size and form of the writing.

No significance.

---

19 PPI

A narrow, angular top and an arcade base.

The concept of self (Ego) is inwardly restricted and rarely allowed to surface.

---

20 i-dots and t-bars

The i-dots are high and rightward.
The t-bars are short and on the stem.

Normal socially, albeit restricted.

---

21 Punctuation

Intelligently used.

Considerate to the reader.
Intelligent response.

22 Signature

Same as script.

No guile. Honest and
straightforward.

23 Lower extensions and loops

Some angular, some straight down,
with pressure.

Sexual feelings restricted.
Strong determination.

24 Dishonesty

There are no indications of
dishonesty.

High integrity.

By completing a full worksheet before compiling your analysis, you will have covered all the factors and, if you have been observant, you should have omitted nothing.

There are no hard and fast rules on the way a compilation of character and personality traits is put together; you will eventually find a way that suits you best. However, as a guide, you must always consider the Form Level first, in order to assess the writer's intelligence level and intellectual capacity as well as his or her spontaneity and reliability rating. Next consider at least five of the dominants and what they represent (for example, size, slant, regularity, degree and form of connection and pressure), to give you a framework on which to apply your findings, then at least five of the less dominant factors (zone measurement, width, shading, margins, PPI) and then the remainder of the worksheet. In this way you will have built up the personality and character analysis. Next, read it carefully and consider whether you have missed anything, taking into account your knowledge to date and your intuition. But it is very important that you do not rely on intuition alone.

After a lot of practice over many months, probably 18 or more, you will begin to realize that the Form Level alone will give you a quick basis for an analysis, providing a thumbnail sketch of the writer if that is all you need, rather than a full and comprehensive analysis which will take a minimum of four hours to complete properly.

If you are taking the subject seriously, I strongly suggest that you consult a qualified teacher. You will then of course develop the analysis in the way the teacher prefers.

THE ANALYSIS

You are now ready to complete the analysis from your worksheet findings. The first thing to remember is never to lose sight of the Form Level. Start by writing a first draft. This will probably start off short, but will increase in length as you gain more experience. Keep to the main issues at first — the report may be short but it will be correct. When I taught graphology, my students wrote a draft of their findings, double spaced, in this order: Emotional Response, Mental and Intellectual Qualities, Social Inclinations, and Working Qualities. These were written out on cards or separate sheets to be combined finally into one assessment. When you are satisfied with this draft, write out the final version, not forgetting negative aspects (of which there may well be some). Report them diplomatically, so as not to offend the recipient, but make them aware that you know their weaknesses as well as their strengths. It is also important that the analysis should be free from jargon; it must be easy to understand.

You will find that reports vary in length, depending upon the script being analysed. For instance, a copybook writer will not be so interesting compared with a writer whose script is original, fast, and merits a high Form Level, on which there will be more personality traits to write about.

Always be aware that a report is confidential, and head it as such. Show it only to the person for whom it is intended and at this early stage ask for their comments. You will make mistakes, but do not be discouraged. To reiterate, never divulge your findings to anyone who happens to ask. Tell them kindly but firmly that you are sorry but you have to respect a confidence. They in turn will respect you for this. Remember also that you should not analyse a signature without a sample of the script, because there could be a variation between the two.

The following example shows the analysis from the work-sheet set out above.

Reference no. 000

CONFIDENTIAL   Date:

This writer has a well-balanced, independent approach to life and, unless put under pressure, is emotionally stable. But under pressure she will become somewhat restless and needs to regain her composure, her control and the cool attitude for which she is known.

Her intellect is average, not brilliant, but practical and reliable, reflecting a common-sense attention to all things and a careful, constructive thinking process. She will need time to assimilate knowledge, but her recall is good. She will therefore remember what she needs to know and what is, to her, important. She is a good organizer and time-keeper, but must be aware of what she is doing at all times to alleviate anxiety.

Her imagination is realistic. She is not inclined towards day-dreaming or wishful thinking. She possesses the ability to reason things out before taking action, and will not rush into a situation without due care and attention. Details matter and must be correct.

She is cautious of others knowing her plans and ideas until she knows they are viable. Her social approach to others is formal, until she gets to know them better. Their values need to be the same as hers – traditional. She also possesses a strong sense of justice. She will be slow to adapt to new ideas until they have been proven to be efficient. A determined person, she would not be influenced by a stronger personality. Her determination to do things her way is purposeful and, when provoked, she can be downright stubborn and will stand her ground against all odds.

She is wary of progressive pursuits, mainly because she is strongly aware of the past and has a very watchful regard for her future.

While she is co-operative, she is not really socially minded; she will introduce herself, then withdraw until she is convinced that the other person's motives are genuine. This applies particularly in a potentially close relationship, in which case she could become possessive. However, there is no marked desire to dominate, nor a wish to project a personality other than what she really is: honest and straightforward, with no grandiose ideas.

Provided her work is financially sound, she has very little ambitious drive. Although she would work within a team, she is also contented and has the initiative to work alone, but without interference. Once settled in, she would be committed to the company and concerned to follow their established patterns of operation: in short, a good all-rounder. A high integrity rating is indicated.

There would be a reluctance to discuss sexual matters initially until a deeply involved and lasting friendship is established.

NOTE: Intimate matters should not be included in an analysis except when the writer is the recipient, or for marriage compatibility, when both people would be assessed and any imbalance likely to cause problems would be discussed intelligently and with understanding.

CONCLUSION

USING GRAPHOLOGY IN EVERYDAY LIFE

With so many things to look for, you may be thinking, 'I'll never do it.' But you will, through practice and – the essential ingredient – experience. Analysing handwriting may even become a compulsion. Any handwriting you see will automatically undergo the treatment – even before you read the actual message.

There will be times when you will need to retrace your steps to refresh your memory, but if you remember the level you were at a few months before, you will be amazed at how much knowledge you have gained during that time. With experience will come confidence in your ability to latch on to a personality without knowing or meeting the writer personally. You will be enthusiastic and eager to become more and more proficient and, after a time of working alone, you will probably think about a professional teacher to bring your accumulated knowledge into an ordered routine. For this, a disciplined approach is necessary, so that you can fully assimilate the learning material you will be given with your lessons. Any problems you have encountered will be explained to you, with a personal progress report and encouragement towards a future in the absorbing subject of handwriting analysis.

I must emphasize, however, that concurrently with your graphology practice you should be studying basic psychology, which will acquaint you with different personality characteristics and help you in your overall knowledge – particularly the psychology of C G Jung. Read also about the four functions, thinking, feeling, sensation and intuition, which relate to all human beings.

USES OF GRAPHOLOGY

Personal use

Graphology can be used for self-knowledge. Ask enquirers if there are any specific areas they particularly want to cover. Do not make any exaggerated claims. Keep the analysis simple, putting the emphasis on the positive aspects of behaviour patterns, allowing them to understand their strengths and weaknesses. It is not wise to cause worry by being too negative, but remember, enquirers will want to know enough to do something about their deficiencies. If possible direct their interest to constructive ideas.

Recruitment use

The technique of graphology is today used professionally, mainly in helping to select personnel for key positions. It is here that the personality is assessed in terms of performance and potential, in relation to the specific demands of the position. It is therefore necessary to obtain a full job specification and to ascertain whether the assessment will be seen by only one person or discussed by other managers at board level. Personal details irrelevant to the job should not be included. Always use a reference number rather than a name, so that only the person for whom the analysis is intended knows the identity of the writer.

Personnel managers and other recruitment staff want straightforward information – direct and factual – so you must be absolutely objective. It is not fair to the management or the candidate if weak points which indicate inadequacy in intellectual, emotional or physical resources are glossed over. The applicant's integrity is also usually an important consideration and should be handled realistically and put into proper context in accordance with its dominance. A reliability and integrity rating of high, average or low will usually get the message across and can perhaps be explained further by telephone.

Some personnel managers ask only for a percentage evaluation of certain requirements, or a rating of high, medium or low, or marks out of 10. While these are helpful, they should be followed by a verbal summary of the candidate's ability and any other points which the percentage evaluation does not cover, but which could be relevant, such as general incompatibility with others or nervousness.

I have found that breaking the report up into sections, such as intellectual qualities, temperament, social tendencies, working qualities and moral values, makes for easier reading if it is a big one. Make your own list of qualities on which to comment. Here are a few examples.

- Reliability
- Responsibility
- Problem-solving initiative
- Self-confidence
- Leadership ability
- Tolerance and patience
- Analytical ability
- Constructiveness in argument
- Administrative ability
- Concentration
- Degree of co-operation
- Spontaneity of mental grasp

Marriage compatibility
Graphology is very useful for supplementing or confirming what is already known in assessing the suitability of a marriage partner. No handwriting assessment should be taken lightly; this area is of the utmost importance to the two people concerned, especially if the enquirer is experiencing problems within an existing marriage.

The first consideration is a full analysis of each partner,

paying strict attention to the variations of outlook and behaviour which, in the close contact of day-to-day life, could come to the fore and create friction and discord, particularly in the more intimate areas of the relationship. For instance, a very thick stroke indicates a sensual need for close bodily contact (see *chapter 3*); a very thin stroke indicates a cool reception to this type of intimate contact. A garland writer (see *chapter 2*) would need a lot of love and affection, while an angular writer would be rather critical of this type of need. Compromise and understanding would be necessary after the problem had been explained.

Such enquirers are most likely to be uncertain of their ability to judge other people, aware of their own shortcomings and doubtful of their ability to adjust. They will want an easily understood report, saying in essence Yes or No. You might suggest that if there is a serious doubt, it would be unwise to proceed. However, there is often only one facet in the intended partner which worries the enquirer. This may be resolved, in which case the way is then clear to make a successful, meaningful relationship.

One must remember that love is a very strong emotion and capable of overcoming obstacles which may otherwise be considered insurmountable. A large number of contented relationships are based on thoughtfulness and tolerance of the needs and desires of the partner, whether they occur in the intellectual, social or instinctual (sexual) area. For example, there are men who, having had domineering mothers, prefer a woman who will exercise a strong hand over them. They may be detached at the office, but sentimental at home. Their writing is very likely to be tall, upright and narrow, but with a very thick stroke quality. There will also be leftward tendencies. The woman's writing is likely to be angular with heavy pressure, indicating dominance.

The special qualities to look for in this area are:

- Mental capacity and balance
- Sexual capacity and balance
- General reliability
- Willingness to co-operate

- Kindness and unselfishness
- Sincerity
- Generosity
- Maturity
- A sense of humour

There should also be some similarity of temperament, outlook, and standards. If you are particularly interested in marriage compatibility, in which graphology can play a rewarding part, I recommend the book *I Do: Your Guide to a Happy Marriage* by Hans J Eysenck (Century 1983). It also includes his chart on temperaments.

Vocational guidance

School leavers may want pointers to career prospects, or more experienced people may wish to change direction. This is one area where we, as graphologists, cannot be specific. We can only point people in a general direction, based on their personality, natural capabilities, ambition and intellectual capacity. Most people have a basic idea of what they would like to do as an occupation and this should be ascertained before the analysis is undertaken. It is the one area where as much as possible should be known about the applicant, to facilitate a better understanding of his or her job prospects. The *Careers Guide*, published by HMSO, is a very useful book in this respect.

You should note that practical experience is absolutely essential before work is attempted in any of these areas. Practise on friends and relatives who will comment on your expertise realistically and honestly so that you can assess your progress. You should spend at least two years on study and practical application before any serious analytical work is undertaken. It is a serious study and, as with other subjects, needs constant and careful attention. You will derive great satisfaction from being told by your friends that you are correct in your assessment of them.

The best way of learning, of course, is to undergo a course of personal tuition with a qualified teacher. Graphology organizations, many of whose addresses are at the back of this book, will put you in touch with a suitable tutor.

You may be asked to give an opinion on an anonymous letter or a suspected forgery. This is a very specialized area of handwriting examination, which requires many years' experience and a specific knowledge beyond the scope of this book. Any enquiries for such work should be passed on to a known practitioner or to The Graphology Society, who will recommend a suitable suspect-document examiner.

Little by little you will take on an awareness of how people's handwriting is a valid means of relating to them fully and gaining their respect with your understanding of their weaknesses as well as their strengths. You will find, I hope, as I have, years of pleasure in your future as a graphologist: I wish you well in your pursuit.

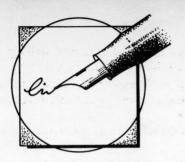

GLOSSARY

Alignment – The spatial organization of the writing on the page

Amplification – The enlarging of the letterforms more than normal

Analysis – The graphological conclusions

Angular – A connective form, characterized by points on the change of direction in a letterform or connection

Arcade – A connection in the shape of an arch, closed at the top

Arrhythmic – Disturbed flow of the overall movement in the rhythmic quality of a handwriting

Baseline – The line, imaginary or actual, on which the writing rests

Calligraphy – The art of beautiful writing

Character trait – One facet of general attitude and behaviour

Connection, degree of – The extent to which individual letters are joined to produce connected writing

Connection, form of – The way in which letters are joined in connected writing, namely arcade, garland, angular, thread, copybook and wavy line (qqv)

Copybook – The style used to teach the basics of handwriting in schools; the connective form which characterizes it

Covering stroke – A stroke which covers another, instead of opening out

Direction – The way in which a line of writing proceeds – in the Western world, left to right

Disconnected script – Writing in which the individual letters of a word are not joined by a connecting stroke, often called printscript

Dominant – One of the main characteristics in the writing analysed

Ego – The conscious inner self, the balance between the conscience and the pleasures of life. The image of oneself

Elaboration – Letterforms written in a fancy style, often tasteless

Evenness – Relating mainly to the regular formation of letters in a word

Flexible – Not rigid in movement

Flourish – A fancy stroke, often in the initial or the signature; can also be at the end of a letter

Form – The shape of letters

Form Level – The overall appearance of a handwriting, the accent being on speed, spacing and the form of the letters; rhythm and originality are a prime factor. It sets the standard from which the traits of the handwriting are judged – positive or negative

Fullness – Describes letters in which more than normal space is evident, mainly in the loops (qv)

Garland – A form of connection in which the letters 'n' and 'm' are open at the top, resembling 'u' and 'w'

Graphology – The study of handwriting to determine the character and personality of the writer

Initial stroke – A pen stroke at the beginning of a letter, not always essential

Loop – A round or oval shape that curves around to cross itself; can be open

Margin – The space left at the sides, top and bottom of a sheet of writing, acting as a frame

Negative – A reaction or behaviour pattern which would not benefit the writer

Ornamentation – An additional embellishment to a letterform, which serves no purpose (except in a calligraphic script)

Pastose – Thick as in a stroke formed by the pen being held at an acute slanting angle; the resultant ink looks as though it is painted on

Positive – A characteristic which benefits the writer; an efficient indication

PPI – The personal pronoun 'I'

Pressure – The depth of the stroke, from which there would be an indentation on the reverse of the paper

Resting dot – A dot formed either by pressure or ink spread when the pen stops the writing movement, while still resting on the paper

Rhythm – The flow of the writing movement which gives life to the overall pattern; an interplay of tension and release

Shading – The contrast between the thick down strokes and the thin up strokes in the handwriting

Sharp – Thin, sharp, as in a stroke with points

Sign – A piece of writing, word or letter indicating a characteristic (a factor)

Signature – A personal sign in whatever form it is manifested; it is a person's mark of recognition – not necessarily legible

Simplified – A piece of writing devoid of superfluous strokes; it must remain legible to be a positive indication

Slant – The inclination of a writing – leftward, upright and rightward

Speed – The tempo of the writing movement

Stroke – A single written line in whatever direction

Temperament – The writer's individual tendencies, relating to the emotions

Tension/release – The muscular action necessary to produce the arm, wrist and finger movements

Thread – A form of connection appearing as a slight wavy line, with no definition

Wavy line – A form of connection with a wavy appearance, but more definition than a thread (see above)

Width – The distance between the strokes of a letter

Zones – The upper, middle and lower parts of a letter; the Western 'f' has all three zones in a single letter

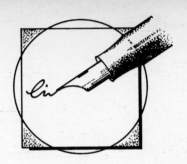

FURTHER READING

Branston, Barry, *Graphology Explained*, Piatkus Books, London, 1989

Gullan-Whur, Margaret, *Discover Graphology*, Aquarian Press, Wellingborough, Northants, 1991

Hargreaves, Gloria and Wilson, Peggy, *A Dictionary of Graphology*, Peter Owen, London, 1983

Huntington, Hartford, *You Are What You Write*, Peter Owen, London, 1975

Jacoby, H J, *Analysis of Handwriting*, British Institute of Graphologists, London, 1991

Koren, Anna, *The Secret Self*, Adama Books, New York, 1987

Marne, Patricia, *Crime and Sex in Handwriting*, Constable, London, 1981

Mendel, Alfred O, *Personality and Handwriting*, Stephen Daye Press, New York, 1947

Nezos, Renna, *Graphology*, Rider, London, 1986

Olyanova, Nadya, *Handwriting Tells*, The Bobbs-Merrill Co., Indianapolis, 1969

Pulver, Dr Max, *The Symbolism of Handwriting*, The British Academy of Graphology, London, 1994

Roman, Klara G, *Handwriting: A Key to Personality*, Pantheon Books, New York, 1952

Saudek, Robert, *Experiments with Handwriting*, Books for Professionals, Sacramento, 1978

Simpson, Diane, *The Analysis of Handwriting, Personality and Character*, A & C Black, London, 1985

Singer, Eric, *A Manual of Graphology*, Duckworth, London, 1987

— *Personality in Handwriting*, Duckworth, London, 1974

Sonnemann, Ulrich, *Handwriting Analysis as a Psychodiagnostic Tool*, Grune & Stratton, New York, 1950

Wolff, Werner, *Diagrams of the Unconscious*, Grune & Stratton, New York, 1948

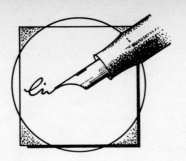

USEFUL ADDRESSES

CANADA

La Société de Spécialistes en Graphologie du Quebec
990 Rue Eymard
Quebec GIS 4A1

Saskatchewan Handwriting Analysis Club
709 Main Street
Saskatoon
Saskatchewan S7H OJ9

EUROPE AND THE MIDDLE EAST

Cercles Européen de Recherches et d´Etudes Graphologiques
Michel De Grave, Director
Avenue Minerve 23B. 25
1190 Bruxelles
BELGIUM

La Société Belge de Graphologie
Avenue de Broqueville 227
1200 Bruxelles
BELGIUM

Fédération Nationale des Graphologues Professionels
2 bis Rue Roger Simon Barboux
94110 Arcueil
FRANCE

Société de Graphologie d´Aquitaine
9 Place du Parlement
33000 Bordeaux
FRANCE

European Association for the Psychology of Writing
PO Box 100803
60008 Frankfurt-am-Main
GERMANY

Internationale Gesellschaft für Dynamische und Klinische Schriftpsychologie (DKS)
c/o Dr Christian Dettweiler
Erlenweg 14
70597 Stuttgart 70
GERMANY

Naftali Institute for Handwriting Analysis
52 Brodezki Street
Ramat Aviv
ISRAEL

Associazione Grafologica Italiana
Via Oberdan 3
60122 Ancona
ITALY

Associazione Italiana Grafoanalisi per l'Eta Evolutiva
Via Renier 25/6
10141 Torino
ITALY

Istituto Grafologica Girolamo Moretti
Piazza San Francisco 7
61029 Urbino (ps)
ITALY

Agrupacion de Grafoanalistas
Avenue de St Antonio
M Clares 446
08027 Barcelona
SPAIN

Associedad Espanola de Grafologica
Apartado 40099
28007 Madrid
SPAIN

Association Grafopsicologica
Pez 27–10 dcha.
28004 Madrid
SPAIN

Svenska Skriftpsykologiska Foreningen
c/o Ragner Kvillmark
Muraragatan 14 A
652 28 Karlstad
SWEDEN

The Academy of Graphology
1 Queen's Elm Square
London SW3 6ED
UK

The British Institute of Graphologists
4th Floor
Bell Court House
11 Blomfield Street
London EC2M 7AY
UK

The Graphology Society
33 Bonningtons
Thriftwood
Hutton
Brentwood
Essex CM13 2TL
UK

Mrs Marion Rayner, MBIG (Dip)
Consultant Graphologist
British Representative of the
Association for Graphological
Studies, USA
Bermuda Lodge
Curley Hill Road
Lightwater
Surrey, GU18 5YH
UK
Tel 01276 474806
Comprehensive
correspondence courses and
personal tuition.

Mrs Anne Cooksey
Bishop's Close
Sonning
Reading
Berkshire RG4 0ST
UK
Tel 01734 692263, fax 01734
692263
For advice on available books
on graphology

Mr Nigel Bradley
91 Hawkesley Avenue
Chesterfield
Derbyshire S40 4TJ
UK
Papers relating to graphology
seminars and studies in
handwriting

USA

American Association of Handwriting Analysts (AAHA)
c/o Rose Matousek
820 West Maple Street
Hinsdale
Illinois 60521
or
35970 Perth
Livonia
Michigan 48154

American Society of Professional Graphologists
Edith Eisenberg –
Corresponding Secretary
9109 North Branch Drive
Bethesda
Maryland 20817

Association of Professional Graphometrists
780 Market Street
No 315
San Francisco
California 94102

Calumet Association for Handwriting Analysts
7210 Knickerbocker Parkway
Hammond
Indiana 46323

Handwriting Analysts International
1504 West 29th Street
Davenport
Iowa 52804

**Independent Texas
Handwriting Analysts'
Association**
12612 Sunglow
Dallas
Texas 75234

**Institute of Graphological
Research**
610 Lochmoor Court
Danville
California 94526

**National Society for
Graphology**
250 West 57th Street
Suite 2032
New York
NY 10107

**Rocky Mountain Graphology
Association**
3053 South Zenobia
Denver
Colorado 80236

**Society for Integrative
Graphology**
535 Perry Street
Sandusky
Ohio 44870

**Society of Handwriting
Analysts**
1127 Twelfth Street
Laurel
Maryland 20810

**The International
Graphological Society**
3153 Spur Trail
Dallas
Texas 75234

INDEX